VATCH'S **THAI KITCHEN**

VATCH'S **THAI KITCHEN**

Thai dishes to cook at home

Vatcharin Bhumichitr

Photography by Peter Cassidy

RYLAND
PETERS
& SMALL

LONDON NEW YORK

Dedication

To my friends

First published in Great Britain in 2005
This paperback edition published in 2008
by Ryland Peters & Small
20–21 Jockey's Fields, London WC1R 4BW
www.rylandpeters.com

10 9 8 7 6 5 4 3 2 1

ISBN 978-1-84597-583-8

A catalogue record for this book
is available from the British Library.

Printed and bound in China

Senior Designer Steve Painter
Commissioning Editor Elsa Petersen-Schepelern
Production Patricia Harrington
Art Director Gabriella Le Grazie
Publishing Director Alison Starling

Food Stylist Linda Tubby
Prop Stylist Róisín Nield
Indexer Hilary Bird

Notes

• All spoon measurements are level unless otherwise stated.

• All herbs are fresh, unless specified otherwise.

• Eggs are large unless otherwise specified. Uncooked or partly cooked eggs should not be served to the very old, frail, young children, pregnant women or those with compromised immune systems.

• Most ingredients will be available in Western supermarkets. Others are widely sold in Chinatown markets and Asian and Oriental stores. To order on-line or by mail order and for a list of specialist outlets, please see page 142.

• Galangal is a popular ingredient in Thai spice pastes and other dishes. It is widely available in markets selling South-east Asian produce. It can be successful frozen and used straight from frozen. A common substitute in the West is fresh ginger, though it has a totally different flavour and the recipes will not taste the same.

(v) Dishes suitable for vegetarians.

contents

YOUR THAI KITCHEN

It was dawn, and I was just waking after the first night in my new house in Ko Samui, Thailand. I remembered waking up as a child in my parents' house in Bangkok. The ground floor of the house was rendered brick, painted a sun-bleached yellow, and the upper floor was timber. It was a big house with balconies on the first floor: at the front they overlooked the garden, at the back they overlooked a courtyard, the maid's house and the kitchen. This is the traditional layout for Thai houses with the kitchen at the back, separated from the house, sometimes linked by a covered walkway. I remember it as the source of the most wonderful smells and food.

My new house in Ko Samui has a similar layout, but it is built entirely of wood. The ground floor has shutters at the front and rear that fold back, so it can be completely open to the breeze. On that first night, I slept on the ground floor with the rear shutters open and when I woke I saw the back courtyard, then beyond the courtyard was the sea, and to the right an empty kitchen.

My first job and pleasure that day was to buy everything for my new kitchen. In this book, I will tell you all that you need to cook Thai food in a Western kitchen. Where I live, I am fortunate that I have to walk only 200 metres and I am in the local market that caters both for Buddhists and the local Muslim fishing community. I doubt that you will have such a selection of foods available to you, but in the following recipes I use ingredients that are generally available in Oriental shops or large supermarkets. Nowadays, almost everything you need to cook authentic Thai food is readily available, and a list of websites and shops selling Thai ingredients and utensils appears on page 142.

ingredients

Coriander *Pak chee*

Coriander is also known as 'cilantro' or Chinese parsley – it is, indeed, a member of the parsley family and much resembles Italian flat leaf parsley. Like its relation, coriander leaves are generally used as a topping in Thailand, whole or chopped up and sprinkled on a finished dish, as much for the visual effect as the flavour.

Coriander root is much used in Thailand – some dishes require a great many roots and this often creates a problem in the West, where suppliers often chop off the root. One solution is to persuade your greengrocer to get some uncut coriander for you, or to look for any bunches with one or two roots still surviving. Alternatively, grow your own. Cut off the roots with about 5 mm of the stalk, wash them carefully and freeze to be used as needed. Although a little wet when thawed, they are perfectly adequate. If you cannot get any roots, then use an extra length of the lower stalks. Coriander leaves are now so easy to find that preservation is hardly necessary – the washed plant will keep for a few days in a refrigerator, either wrapped in a plastic bag or in a salad compartment.

Sweet basil *Bai horabha*
and Holy basil *Bai krapow*

Both of these are, in fact, varieties of sweet basil. The herb we call 'sweet' basil is nearest to the one used in Italian cuisine. Holy basil, with narrower leaves and sometimes a reddish-purple tinge, has a stronger, more intense taste and must be cooked to release its flavour.

There is a third Thai basil, *bai manglak* or lemon-scented basil, which has slightly hairy, paler green leaves. It is delicious, but very fragile and it cannot be exported easily, so you are unlikely to find it outside Thailand.

The more robust sweet and holy basils can be dried and do not have to be soaked before using. While some of the flavour will be lost in the drying process, it is the only way to preserve basil, because the delicate leaves will be damaged if frozen.

Lemongrass *Takrai*

In its natural state, lemongrass is exactly that – a grass, easily recognized by its long, lemon-scented blades. In warm climates, it grows quickly and abundantly, one stalk multiplying to almost 50 in a single season. It will occasionally produce a flower, but even in Thailand this is rare.

Lemongrass is found throughout South-east Asia, India, Central and South America and the Caribbean. It can be cultivated under hothouse conditions in temperate climates, but needs great care.

When you find it in a market, the grassy leaves will have been chopped off. What remains is the lower stalk from which the coarsest outer leaves will have been stripped. The pale green, almost white, bulbous stalk then looks something like a fat spring onion or a small leek.

Lime, Kaffir lime and Kaffir lime leaf
Manao, Magrut, Bai magrut

From a cook's point of view, the essential difference between the light green lime, familiar in the West, and the darker, knobbly kaffir, or wild lime, is juice – the kaffir lime doesn't have any. While all of a lime, zest and juice, is used, only the zest of the kaffir lime is serviceable. The reason kaffir lime is so much liked in Thailand is that its zest has a far more intense flavour than its lighter cousin. Indeed, we tend to think that there is little difference between a lemon and an ordinary lime (we use the same word, *manao*, for both). You can peel a kaffir lime and freeze the zest for future use.

We also use the leaves of the kaffir lime as a herb. They are much appreciated for the pungent lemony aroma they give to a dish. They too can be frozen or dried, and are used in the way that bay leaves are in the West. Unless otherwise specified, the kaffir lime leaves in the recipes in this book are fresh. Where dry leaves are used, they need not be soaked but can be put straight into the mixture in the same way as bay leaves.

Small red or green chillies
Prik khee noo suan

The Thai name for these tiny red or green chillies (about 1.25 cm long) means 'mouse droppings'. They are much appreciated for their intense heat. Because they do not keep well, you are unlikely to find them outside South-east Asia, because exporters prefer to send the next largest size.

Bird's eye chillies
Pri khee noo

Slightly larger bird's eye chillies, at about 2.5 cm long, are marginally less hot, but still pretty fiendish.

Large red or green chillies
Prik chee faa

These fresh red or green chillies are 7.5–10 cm long. They are slightly less hot than the small ones.

Garlic *Kratiam*

Garlic is an essential part of most Thai dishes. It is used whole, chopped, crushed, raw, fried and pickled. Thai garlic cloves are small with a thin papery skin, which is why we often do no more than crush them with a heavy blow from the side of a cleaver before tossing them, skins included, into the pan. With non-Thai garlic you will have to peel off the skin.

The first use of garlic in Thai cooking is to flavour the cooking oil before frying meat or vegetables. We never use oils that carry their own flavour, such as olive oil, and only rarely use sesame oil. Mostly we prefer bland vegetable oils, such as peanut oil.

Some dishes call for garlic to be fried in a little oil until golden brown, then reserved to be sprinkled over the finished dish, almost like a final pungent condiment.

Usually, garlic is a hidden flavour, but sometimes it moves to centre stage, cut into ovals and deep-fried to add a rich taste and crisp texture. Where a really strong flavour is required, we use pickled garlic.

Buy garlic that is firm to the touch and seems heavy for its size – a slight pinkish tinge is a good sign. Garlic keeps well in a cool, dry and well-ventilated place, but should not be stored in the refrigerator where it may become mildewed or start to sprout.

Shallots *Hom daeng*

The shallot is a sweeter and milder member of the onion family. Thai shallots are so sweet we sometimes use them in sweet dishes. Shallots are best when small, with coppery-pink skins, which should be peeled like ordinary onions. Some varieties come in tight clusters like large garlic cloves, and must be pulled apart. Avoid the very large varieties that sometimes appear, because these can be as strongly flavoured as the average onion, which rather misses the point. Small shallots are sold loose or tied in bundles. They should be firm and without any sprouts or blemishes or signs of rot. Like garlic, they keep well in a cool, dry, well-ventilated place, but may sprout in the refrigerator.

Ginger *King*

Ginger, often called 'root ginger' or 'ginger root', was until recently more often seen as preserved sweet ginger in jars or as ground ginger, which could be rather musty and unpleasant. Fortunately, the knobbly, golden-beige 'fingers' of fresh ginger are now quite common in markets and supermarkets.

An infusion of ginger and water is good for stomach disorders, including morning sickness during pregnancy. It is also taken as a stimulant.

There are several varieties of ginger grown in Thailand, each with its own unique properties. Young fresh ginger is also available and is still tender enough to be stir-fried like a vegetable. In Thai cuisine, ginger is often eaten raw as a spicy nibble with dips or sausages. For this purpose, use only the youngest, tenderest rhizomes – older ginger is too fibrous and dry, although it is quite acceptable if cooked. Recipes usually recommend that you peel a piece of fresh ginger, then sliver it into thin matchsticks so it will cook thoroughly and be easily digestible.

If you find any young ginger (it will be more pink in colour) you should rush to buy it. Whether young or old, choose roots that are firm and not shrivelled or marked. Wrapped well in clingfilm, ginger can be kept in the refrigerator for up to 2 weeks.

Galangal *Khaa*

This rhizome was immensely popular in late medieval Europe, but has not been much used in Western cooking since. It is now returning,

thanks to the popularity of Oriental cuisines. Like its cousin ginger, it is good for stomach problems, especially nausea. While slightly harder than ginger, it is used in exactly the same way – peeled and slivered into matchsticks or finely sliced into thin rounds in order to cook thoroughly.

Galangal is widely available in markets selling South-east Asian produce. Fresh ginger is used as a common substitute in the West, though it has a totally different flavour and the recipes will not taste the same.

Well wrapped, galangal will keep in the refrigerator for 2 weeks, or it can be frozen and used from frozen.

Coconut cream and milk *Ma prow*

Coconut cream and its thinner form, coconut milk, are available from a number of sources. Authentically, of course, they are made from fresh mature coconuts, but there are a number of short cuts. You can buy blocks of coconut, which are not unlike blocks of white wax; these are heated according to the instructions on the packet and dissolve into a cream. You can also buy powdered coconut milk, which again includes instructions on adding water to produce the desired liquid mixture. I cannot really recommend either of these products, because the manufacturers tend to adulterate the coconut with flour, and this produces a somewhat stale flavour. By far the best short cut is to use cans or cartons of coconut cream or milk, which are easily available and made from fresh mature coconuts. Some brands do add a little flour, but not enough to spoil the flavour. If a recipe specifies coconut cream, and you have only coconut milk, don't shake the can. When opened, you will find it separated into thick cream at one end, and thinner milk at the other. Carefully spoon off the cream for use in the recipe.

Fish sauce *Nam pla*

This is the main flavouring in Thai cooking, for which there is no substitute. It is the same salty seasoning used in Ancient Rome where a similar liquid called 'garum' or 'liquamen' was used before it was replaced by salt. Although it can also be made with shrimp, fish sauce is most commonly the thin brown liquid extracted from salted, fermented fish. The best is home-made and is a light whisky colour with a refreshing salty taste rather than being dark, with a heavy, bitter tang and a powerful fishy aroma.

When buying commercially produced fish sauce, I try to find a lighter rather than a darker liquid. Colour is also the best way to judge whether a bottle has been open for too long, because the sauce darkens with age. It should be discarded if it has changed colour significantly. Other than that, there is little to choose between the different producers and their country of origin – Thailand, Vietnam and China all produce good fish sauce. While some people prefer not to buy it in plastic containers, I doubt whether that makes any difference – go by the colour if anything.

Light and dark soy sauce *Siew*

These are Chinese sauces made from salted, cooked soya beans fermented with flour, after which the liquid is extracted. There are several varieties and, while all are 'meaty' in flavour, they vary in colour and intensity from light to dark brown or almost black. Commercially, only two varieties are available: light soy sauce, which is thin with a clear, delicate flavour, mild enough to be used as a condiment at table, and dark soy sauce which is thicker with a stronger, sweeter flavour, having been fermented with other ingredients such as mushrooms and ginger that darken the final liquid. However, the difference between light and dark is slight, with dark being used more to colour the food than anything. If you rarely cook Oriental food, you will probably need only a bottle of the more common light soy sauce.

Oyster sauce *Nam man hoy*

This thick brown liquid is also of Chinese origin and is made from oysters that have been cooked in soy sauce and then mixed with seasonings and brine. The result does not, however, taste of fish, as might be expected. It is sold in bottles and somewhat resembles brown ketchup. If used rarely, it should be stored in the refrigerator.

Bean sauce *Tow jiew*

Bean sauces consist of slightly mashed fermented soya beans – black or yellow. They help thicken a dish as well as add flavour. Black bean sauce is thick and deeply coloured and is used to give a richer flavour than even dark soy sauce can achieve.

Yellow bean sauce is more salty and pungent, but again, this is a quite subtle refinement. If you cook Thai food only occasionally, you may need no more than a jar of black bean sauce. You can, however, get very small cans of both sauces, sufficient for one Thai cooking session. If you can get it only in larger jars, preservation offers no problems as both bean sauces will keep almost indefinitely in the refrigerator.

Chilli sauce *Sod prik*

A thick dipping sauce made from a combination of sweet and hot chillies, pulped and mixed with vinegar, garlic and other spices.

Chilli powder *Prik pon*

A red powder made by grinding small dried red chillies (*prik khee noo haeng*). In Thailand it is sold in jars, packets or cardboard containers.

Shrimp paste *Kapee*

Because it is full of protein and is a good source of vitamin B, shrimp paste is a staple for many of Asia's poor people, whose diet consists of boiled rice flavoured with this pungent preserve. The paste is made by pounding shrimp with salt and leaving them to decompose. It is sold both dried and 'fresh', a slight misnomer when what is really meant is 'not dried'.

The 'fresh' *kapee* is shrimp pink and can be bought in jars in the West, though it is difficult to find. It can be stored in the refrigerator. The sun-dried variety is dark purple from the black eyes of the kheu shrimp, but be wary if it is too dark as this may mean that dye has been added. Dried *kapee* is stronger than fresh, but once again it should not be painfully salty. It can be kept without refrigerating. Rayong produces the best dried *kapee*.

Both fresh and dried shrimp paste have a disturbingly powerful aroma and you should remove what you want from the jar as quickly as possible in case the bad smells escape into your kitchen. Fortunately this odour disappears when the *kapee* is cooked.

You can use either fresh or dried shrimp paste in a recipe. Unless otherwise stated, my recipes all call for dried *kapee*. If substituting fresh, use double the quantity of dried. If none can be found you could use Western anchovy paste – about half the amount of the dried shrimp paste required.

Dried shrimp *Gung haeng*

These are not preserved shrimp waiting to be reconstituted in water and used as a seafood ingredient in a dish. Instead they should be considered more as a dry flavouring that is especially good with blander ingredients such as cabbage and bean curd. Ideally, dried shrimp should be tiny, a natural shrimp pink and not too salty. This flavouring is made by boiling and peeling shrimp, then spreading them out in the sun to dry. The end result is sold loose, in jars or plastic bags. Dried shrimp can be kept for a long time, though they may turn slightly moist, in which case they must be either sun-dried again or dry-heated briefly in the oven.

Look out for a special version from the southern Thai city of Songkla. These shrimp are not peeled but are dried in their shells. They are good deep-fried, after which the shells become crisp and edible, ready to be served as a appetizer.

Palm sugar *Nam tan peep*

Palm sugar is produced from the sap of various kinds of palm. The commonest are the coconut palm and the sugar palm, each of which gives a slightly different flavour, though the standard commercial product, sold in cans or cakes, has a fairly uniform taste. The unique quality of palm sugar is its deep caramel flavour, quite different from ordinary cane sugar.

If coconut sap is left to ferment for just a day you get palm wine or palm toddy, a highly alcoholic beverage. If the sap is boiled down until it crystallizes, you get a coarse sticky sugar. The deep flavour of palm sugar adds a distinctive edge to Thai confections, but it is also used to add another dimension to savoury dishes such as curries.

If you plan to use only a little at a time, you should try to buy well-compressed cakes of palm sugar, because these will keep for a long time in a well-sealed jar. The best is soft brown in colour and has a distinctive toffee-like aroma. You should be able to find it without difficulty in Oriental stores or by mail order (page 142).

RICE *Khao*
Fragrant Thai rice (jasmine rice)

These are the names under which Thai rice is sold abroad. It is a long grain, jasmine-scented rice and is of the highest quality. It is served boiled or steamed and can be reheated in a variety of ways, most often fried.

BOILED RICE *KHAO SUAY*

500 g (625 ml) fragrant Thai rice
600 ml water

An experienced Thai cook varies the water according to the age and dryness of the rice, but the above is a reasonable average ratio.

Rinse the rice thoroughly at least 3 times in cold water until the water runs clear. Put the rice in a heavy saucepan and add the water. Cover and quickly bring to the boil. Uncover and cook, stirring vigorously, until the water level is below that of the rice (the surface will begin to look dry). Turn the heat as low as possible, cover the pan again (put a layer of foil under the lid, if necessary, to ensure a tight fit) and steam for 20 minutes.

The good news is that none of this is really necessary. Buy a rice cooker: they are cheap, super-efficient, and make and keep perfect rice with absolutely no fuss or bother.

Sticky or glutinous rice

This is a broad, short grain rice, mostly white, although sometimes brown or even black. As its name implies, it is the opposite of light and fluffy, being thick and almost porridgy. It is the staple of northern Thailand where during a meal it is plucked with the fingers, rolled into a ball and used to scoop up the other food.

Sticky rice is also used throughout Thailand to make sweet dishes, and it is milled into rice flour, which is bought ready-ground.

Sticky rice cannot be cooked in an electric rice-steamer and must be soaked before cooking.

STEAMED STICKY RICE *KHAO NIEW*

500 g (625 ml) glutinous or sticky rice

Soak the rice in water to cover for at least 3 hours or overnight. Drain and rinse thoroughly.

Line the perforated part of a steamer with a double thickness of muslin and add the soaked rice. Heat water in the bottom of the steamer to boiling, then steam the rice over moderate heat for 30 minutes.

utensils

It is quite easy to cook Thai food using utensils available in most Western kitchens: a frying pan instead of a wok, a blender instead of a mortar and pestle, steaming rice in a pan rather than using a rice cooker and so on. If, after trying a few recipes, you decide that you are going to cook Thai food on a more regular basis, it would be wise to invest in some more specialized equipment. This will just make cooking Thai food easier, and more fun.

The basic equipment for setting up a Thai kitchen would be:

- a wok
- a wooden spatula
- a rice cooker
- a wooden chopping block
- a cleaver
- a stone mortar and pestle for crushing herbs and chillies and making pastes.

There are many other "speciality" items, but these will give you a good basis. However, it is not necessary to have these items in order to cook Thai food.

STARTERS AND
PARTY BITES

Thai dips are mostly made from chillies. You find them in all regions of Thailand – served with raw or boiled vegetables, sticky rice in the north and steamed rice in the Central Regions. This dip, as its name implies, is made from young, green, strongly flavoured chillies and is wonderful to serve with drinks at parties. In Thailand, dips are used both as dipping sauces, and as sauces for spooning over rice or other dishes, and this is how I have used them in this book.

vegetables with spicy dip of young chillies

nam prik num

4 large fresh green chillies

4 small fresh green chillies

6 large garlic cloves

6 pink Thai shallots or 3 regular ones

4 medium tomatoes

2 tablespoons freshly squeezed lime or lemon juice

2 tablespoons light soy sauce

½ teaspoon salt

2 teaspoons sugar

to serve

your choice of crisp lettuce, cucumber, radishes, celery or other raw or blanched vegetables

kitchen foil

serves 4

Wrap the chillies, garlic, shallots and tomatoes in foil and put under a preheated medium grill. Cook until they begin to soften, turning once or twice. Unwrap, then pound with a mortar and pestle to form a liquid paste.

Add the lemon juice, soy sauce, salt and sugar to the paste, stirring well, then spoon into a small dipping bowl.

Serve as a dipping sauce, surrounded by crisp salad ingredients, such as lettuce, cucumber, radish and celery, or with raw or blanched vegetables.

Note In Thailand, we never discard the seeds from chillies, but you can do so if you wish. All chillies vary in heat, so we always work to taste, using more or less, according to our preference.

This recipe originates in the Central Regions of Thailand. It has a richer mix of ingredients, and so would have been a dish found in richer families, possibly of Chinese extraction, because we can see Chinese influence in the use of yellow bean sauce. It has a mild sweetness and is less hot than northern dishes. The recipe makes a crisp, fresh starter for a Thai meal, but is also good to serve with drinks before dinner or for parties.

crudités with spicy yellow bean sauce dip

tow jiew lon

crisp vegetables of your choice, such as Belgian endive (chicory), lettuce hearts, green beans and asparagus

spicy yellow bean sauce dip

2 tablespoons yellow bean sauce, drained to remove excess liquid

250 ml coconut milk

4 small shallots, finely chopped

125 g minced pork

125 g minced prawns

2 tablespoons lemon or lime juice

2 teaspoons sugar

1 tablespoon Thai fish sauce

2 large fresh red chillies, sliced lengthways into fine matchsticks

serves 4

To make the crudités, separate or slice the vegetables into small, convenient portions, arrange on a serving platter and set aside. If using vegetables such as beans and asparagus, blanch them in a saucepan of boiling salted water first, then cool under cold water.

To make the dip, use a mortar and pestle to pound the drained yellow beans briefly to break them up a little. Set aside.

Put the coconut milk in a saucepan and heat, stirring until smooth – do not let boil. Add the mashed yellow beans and stir well. Add the shallots, pork, prawns, lemon juice, sugar and fish sauce. Bring to the boil and simmer briefly. Remove from the heat, transfer to a food processor and pulse to blend coarsely. Stir in the chilli matchsticks, pour into a bowl and serve with the crudités.

While I am not a vegetarian myself, this vegetarian dish is a favourite at parties. Thai people consider sesame seeds good for the hair – regular consumption is said keep it strong and shiny, and possibly even maintain the natural blackness longer. Perhaps other hair colours would also benefit.

60 g small button mushrooms, halved

1 small sweet potato, halved lengthways and sliced

2–3 small carrots, halved lengthways

2–3 small courgettes, sliced diagonally

a handful of basil leaves

peanut or sunflower oil, for deep-frying

batter

125 g plain flour

½ teaspoon salt

2 eggs

1 tablespoon sesame seeds

dipping sauce

4 tablespoons light soy sauce

½ teaspoon sugar

1 teaspoon coarsely chopped coriander leaves

1 teaspoon finely chopped fresh ginger

an electric deep-fryer (optional)

serves 4

vegetable fritters with sesame seeds
pak chup bang tod

To make the batter, put the flour and salt in a bowl and mix well. Break the egg into the bowl, add the sesame seeds and mix thoroughly. Gradually add about 300 ml water, whisking constantly. You should have a batter with the thickness of cream.

Heat the peanut oil in a wok or deep-fryer until a light haze appears. Dip each vegetable into the batter, making sure it is thoroughly coated, then slip it into the hot oil. Deep-fry until golden brown. Remove from the oil with a slotted spoon, drain on paper towels, then arrange on a serving dish.

To make the dipping sauce, put the soy sauce, sugar, coriander and ginger in a bowl and stir well. Serve with the vegetables.

People have largely forgotten that this so-called traditional Thai dish originated in India. As a child, I remember it being sold by the Indian community. However, it has been adapted to suit the Thai taste by the addition of more fresh chillies. It is a beautiful and elegant dish of many fascinating flavours. Even better – it is easy to make, and your vegetarian guests will be delighted that you have catered for them so deliciously.

deep-fried yellow bean balls with thick sweet sauce

baa yir

250 g dried split mung beans, soaked in water for 30 minutes and drained

1 tablespoon plain flour

1 teaspoon Red Curry Paste (page 141)

2 tablespoons light soy sauce

2 teaspoons sugar

5 kaffir lime leaves, rolled into a cylinder and finely sliced into slivers

peanut or sunflower oil, for deep-frying

thick sweet sauce

4 tablespoons sugar

6 tablespoons rice vinegar

½ teaspoon salt

an electric deep-fryer (optional)

serves 4

To make the sauce, put the sugar, vinegar and salt in a small saucepan or wok and heat gently until the sugar dissolves. Let cool before serving with the bean balls.

To make the balls, pound the drained mung beans with a mortar and pestle or use a blender to form a coarse paste. Stirring well after each addition, add the flour, curry paste, soy sauce, sugar and lime leaves. Pluck a small piece of the paste and form into a ball the size of a walnut. Do not mould too tightly.

Fill a wok or deep-fryer one-third full with the oil or to the manufacturer's recommended level. Heat until a scrap of noodle will puff up immediately.

Working in batches if necessary, add the balls and fry until golden brown. Remove with a slotted spoon, drain and serve with the thick sweet sauce.

Everywhere in Thailand, fish cakes are a favourite traditional dish. While they are simple to make, they are an excellent benchmark of the good Thai cook. With a bit of practice, you will be able to create a cake of just the right texture and consistency of ingredients. In the old days, the fish and curry paste would have been pounded by hand for a long time with a mortar and pestle, until the cook was happy that the mix was perfect. These days, we can use modern equipment like blenders and food processors and still produce a delicious and aromatic dish.

fish cakes
tod man pla

500 g white fish fillets, such as cod, coley, haddock or monkfish

2 tablespoons Red Curry Paste (page 141)

2 tablespoons Thai fish sauce

60 g thin green beans or Chinese longbeans, very finely sliced

5 kaffir lime leaves, finely chopped

peanut or sunflower oil, for frying

cucumber relish

250 ml rice vinegar

2 tablespoons sugar

5 cm piece of cucumber (unpeeled), coarsely chopped

1 small carrot, chopped

3 shallots, finely sliced

1 medium fresh red chilli, finely sliced

1 tablespoon crushed roasted peanuts (optional)

an electric deep-fryer (optional)

makes 20 cakes

To make the relish, put the vinegar and sugar in a saucepan and heat, stirring until the sugar dissolves. Boil to produce a thin syrup. Remove from the heat and let cool.

When the syrup is cool, add the cucumber, carrot, shallots, chilli and peanuts, if using. Mix thoroughly and set aside.

To mince the fish, cut the fillets into pieces and put in a food processor or blender. Pulse to form a smooth paste, then transfer to a large bowl.

Put the curry paste in the bowl and, using your fingers, blend thoroughly with the minced fish. Add the fish sauce, green beans and kaffir lime leaves and knead together. Shape into small flat cakes about 5 cm across and 1.25 cm thick.

Fill a wok or deep-fryer one-third full with the oil or to the manufacturer's recommended level. Heat until a scrap of noodle will puff up immediately.

Working in batches if necessary, add the fish cakes and fry until golden on both sides. Remove with a slotted spoon and drain on kitchen paper.

Serve the fish cakes with the cucumber relish.

This is one of the most popular starters in my restaurants. I think it is the best combination of prawns and corn and is the first choice when it comes to recommending a starter. You can buy plum sauce, but this one is easy to make and goes with many other dishes.

prawn and corn cakes with plum sauce

tod man kung khao pod

20 black peppercorns

3 garlic cloves

½ teaspoon salt

250 g peeled raw prawns, deveined and finely chopped

fresh corn kernels from 3 uncooked ears of corn

1 tablespoon Thai fish sauce

1 teaspoon sugar

peanut or sunflower oil, for deep-frying

plum sauce

2 pickled plums

125 ml rice vinegar

6 tablespoons sugar

2 small fresh red and green chillies, finely chopped

an electric deep-fryer (optional)

serves 4

To make the sauce, use a fork to scrape the plum flesh from the stone. Put the vinegar in a saucepan, heat gently, then add the sugar and the plum flesh, stirring until the sugar dissolves. Simmer until a thin syrup begins to form, then remove from the heat. Stir in the chillies, then pour into a bowl and set aside.

Using a large mortar and pestle, pound the peppercorns, garlic and salt to form a paste. Add the prawns and pound well into the paste. Add the corn, fish sauce and sugar and pound well. Alternatively, use a food processor.

You should now have a thick paste. Mould the paste into 12 round cakes.

Fill a wok or deep-fryer one-third full with the oil or to the manufacturer's recommended level. Heat until a scrap of noodle will puff up immediately.

Working in batches if necessary, fry the cakes until golden brown, then remove with a slotted spoon, drain on kitchen paper and serve with the plum sauce.

Note Though you can buy ready-made plum sauce, you can make your own with pickled plums available in jars from Oriental markets and by mail order (page 142).

Prawns wrapped in crispy noodles produce a delicious combination – the contrast between the softness of the prawns and the crisp texture of deep-fried noodles is exceptional. Though this dish looks spectacular, it is not difficult to make. In fact, it's a recipe for the home cook, because it has to be wrapped and fried at the last minute, and doesn't lend itself to the large quantities and advance preparation methods of restaurant chefs.

prawns wrapped in crispy noodles
gung sarong

1 egg
½ teaspoon salt
½ teaspoon sugar
1½ teaspoons freshly ground white pepper
8 king prawns, peeled and deveined, tails on
1 nest fresh ba mee noodles
peanut or sunflower oil, for deep-frying

sweet and hot sauce
4 tablespoons sugar
6 tablespoons rice vinegar
½ teaspoon salt
2 small red chillies, finely chopped

an electric deep-fryer (optional)

makes 8: serves 4

To make the sauce, put the sugar, vinegar and salt in a saucepan and heat, stirring until the sugar dissolves. Add the chillies and 4 tablespoons water, stir well and simmer until it becomes a thin syrup. Pour into a dipping bowl.

Put the egg, salt, sugar and pepper in a bowl and beat well. Add the prawns and mix well. Lift 3–4 strands of noodle and wrap each prawn, winding the strands into a mesh thickly covering the prawn.

Fill a wok or deep-fryer one-third full with the oil or to the manufacturer's recommended level. Heat until a scrap of noodle will puff up immediately.

Working in batches if necessary, fry the wrapped prawns until golden brown. Drain and serve with the sweet and hot sauce or plum sauce (page 24).

Note Ba mee noodles are made from egg and wheat flour and are always sold fresh in 'nests'. Buy them in Chinese or South-east Asian markets.

This fascinating dish consists of crab, prawns and pork blended into a fusion of different textures. It is a perfect party dish because it sounds and looks interesting – but most importantly, it tastes delicious. Ready-cracked crab claws are sold in Oriental stores, some fishmongers and by mail order (page 142) – they are too fiddly to crack yourself.

deep-fried crab claws with pork and prawns

poo tod

125 g minced pork

125 g raw prawns, shelled, deveined and finely chopped

1 egg, beaten

2 garlic cloves, finely chopped

1 tablespoon Thai fish sauce

1 tablespoon oyster sauce

1 teaspoon cornflour

½ teaspoon freshly ground white pepper

8 prepared cocktail crab claws (see recipe introduction)

peanut or sunflower oil, for deep-frying

Plum Sauce, to serve (page 24)

an electric deep-fryer (optional)

makes 8: serves 4

Put the pork, prawns, egg, garlic, fish sauce, oyster sauce, cornflour and pepper in a bowl.

Divide the mixture by the number of crab claws (8) and mould one portion around the meaty section of each claw, leaving the pincer exposed.

Fill a wok or deep-fryer one-third full with the oil or to the manufacturer's recommended level. Heat until a scrap of noodle will puff up immediately.

Working in batches if necessary, add the coated crab claws, and deep-fry until the moulded sections are a deep golden brown. Remove with a slotted spoon, drain and serve with the plum sauce.

For this dish only the thick part of the wings (little drumsticks) are used, marinated in a blend of lemongrass and chilli. The crunchiness of the deep-fried lemongrass on the little drumsticks makes for an interesting texture. The winglets are simple to prepare. Run a knife around the narrow end of the wing, just below the knuckle, then use your knife to cut and push the flesh down the bone to form a little ball at the bottom. The bone then acts as a handle, making perfect finger food. This recipe is one of my own creation.

chicken wings with lemongrass and sweet and hot sauce

gai ta-krai

3 stalks of lemongrass, finely chopped

2 small chillies, finely chopped

3 tablespoons oyster sauce

1 tablespoon Thai fish sauce

1 teaspoon sugar

500 g chicken winglets
(also known as drumettes)

peanut or sunflower oil, for deep frying

to serve

Sweet and Hot Sauce (page 27)

sprigs of coriander

an electric deep-fryer (optional)

serves 4

Put the lemongrass, chillies, oyster sauce, fish sauce and sugar in a bowl and beat with a fork. Add the chicken winglets, turn to coat and set aside to marinate for 15 minutes.

Fill a wok or deep-fryer one-third full with the oil or to the manufacturer's recommended level. Heat until a scrap of noodle will puff up immediately.

Working in batches if necessary, fry the chicken wings until golden brown. Remove with a slotted spoon, drain and serve with sweet and hot sauce and sprigs of coriander.

Note If you are unable to find chicken winglets, buy the whole wings and cut off the last 2 joints. Use them for another recipe or to make stock.

Thai food has become increasingly popular in the West, and is even served in English pubs! Chicken satay is one of the most popular Thai dishes on any menu. You can use it as part of a barbecue menu, whether Oriental or not, or as a party snack – the sticks make this very easy to nibble with drinks, and the peanut sauce is good as a dip with other foods, such as crudités.

chicken satay
satay

2 teaspoons coriander seeds
2 teaspoons cumin seeds
4 skinless chicken breasts
2 tablespoons Thai fish sauce
1 teaspoon salt
4 tablespoons peanut or sunflower oil
1 tablespoon curry powder
1 tablespoon ground turmeric
125 ml coconut milk
3 tablespoons sugar
lemon or lime wedges, to serve

peanut sauce
2 tablespoons peanut or sunflower oil
3 garlic cloves, finely chopped
1 tablespoon Panaeng Curry Paste (page 141)
125 ml coconut milk
250 ml chicken stock
1 tablespoon sugar
1 teaspoon salt
2 tablespoons lemon or lime juice
4 tablespoons crushed roasted peanuts

*18–20 cm wooden skewers,
soaked in cold water for about 30 minutes*

serves 4

To make the peanut sauce, heat the oil in a frying pan until a light haze appears. Add the chopped garlic and fry until golden brown. Add the curry paste, mix well and cook for a few seconds. Add the coconut milk, mix well and cook for a few seconds more. Add the stock, sugar, salt and lemon juice. Cook for 1–2 minutes, constantly stirring. Add the ground peanuts, stir thoroughly and pour the sauce into a bowl.

To make the satays, toast the coriander and cumin seeds gently in a small frying pan without oil for about 5 minutes, stirring and shaking to make sure they don't burn. Remove from the heat and grind with a mortar and pestle to make a fine powder. (You could substitute ready-ground seeds if that is more convenient.)

Using a sharp knife, cut the chicken breasts lengthways into thin strips, about 5 mm wide. Put them in a bowl and add the ground toasted seeds, fish sauce, salt, peanut oil, curry powder, turmeric, coconut milk and sugar. Mix thoroughly and refrigerate for at least 8 hours or overnight (you can prepare them in the morning to serve in the evening).

Preheat an overhead grill, charcoal grill or barbecue. Thread 2 pieces of the marinated chicken onto each skewer – not straight through the meat, but rather as if you were gathering or smocking a piece of fabric in a zigzag fashion. Grill the satays until the meat is cooked through – about 6–8 minutes – turning to make sure they are browned on both sides. Serve with the peanut sauce and perhaps a few lemon or lime wedges.

I well remember this dish as one of my father's favourites – my mother often prepared it as an afternoon snack. It makes excellent finger food for parties and often appears on Thai restaurant menus as a starter. It can be served on its own or alternatively with a hot sauce to add a more spicy flavour.

pork toasts
kanom bang na moo

6 slices of white bread, crusts trimmed and each slice cut into 4

4 small garlic cloves, finely chopped

3 coriander roots, chopped

250 g minced pork

1 egg

2 tablespoons Thai fish sauce

a pinch of freshly ground white pepper

peanut or sunflower oil, for deep-frying

to serve

coriander leaves

about 5 cm cucumber, quartered lengthways, then thinly sliced crossways

1 fresh red chilli, finely sliced into rings

a baking sheet

an electric deep-fryer (optional)

serves 4

Preheat the oven to 120°C (250°F) Gas ½. Arrange the pieces of bread on a baking sheet, put in the oven for 5 minutes, then remove.

Meanwhile, using a mortar and pestle or blender, either pound or grind the garlic and coriander roots together. Put in a bowl, then add the pork, egg, fish sauce and white pepper and mix thoroughly. Put 1 teaspoon of the mixture on each piece of toast.

Fill a wok or deep-fryer one-third full with the oil or to the manufacturer's recommended level. Heat until a scrap of noodle will puff up immediately.

Working in batches of 2–3 at a time, fry the toasts for 2–3 minutes until browned. Remove with a slotted spoon, drain on kitchen paper, arrange on a large plate and serve with the coriander leaves, cucumber and chilli.

This is a traditional dish from the north-east of Thailand and goes especially well with Sticky Rice (page 11) and Papaya Salad with Squid (page 54). The marinade of coriander seeds and roots helps to create a uniquely sweet flavour. For best results, the pork is cooked over charcoal, so makes an ideal dish for barbecues. Otherwise cook under an overhead grill or on a stove-top grill pan.

skewered marinated pork
moo ping

1 teaspoon coriander seeds

4 garlic cloves, finely chopped

6 coriander roots, finely chopped

4 tablespoons Thai fish sauce

2 tablespoons light soy sauce

250 ml thick coconut cream

2 tablespoons peanut or sunflower oil

1 tablespoon sugar

½ teaspoon freshly ground white pepper

500 g lean pork, thinly sliced into pieces about 4 x 7.5 cm

lettuce, parsley or coriander, to serve

sauce

2 tablespoons Thai fish sauce

2 tablespoons lemon or lime juice

1 tablespoon light soy sauce

1 teaspoon chilli powder

1 tablespoon sugar

1 tablespoon coarsely chopped fresh coriander leaves

12 long wooden skewers, 15–20 cm, soaked in cold water for at least 30 minutes

makes 12 skewers: serves 4–12

Using a mortar and pestle, pound the coriander seeds, garlic and coriander roots together in turn to form a paste. Then mix in the fish sauce, soy sauce, coconut cream, oil, sugar and pepper until thoroughly blended. Add the pork and stir well, making sure that each piece is thoroughly coated. Let stand for at least 30 minutes, but longer if possible.

To make the sauce, while the meat is marinating, put the fish sauce, lemon juice, soy sauce, chilli powder, sugar and coriander in a small bowl and mix well. Taste – if too hot, add more fish sauce, lemon juice and sugar.

Preheat an overhead grill. Thread 2 pieces of meat onto each skewer, making sure that as much of the surface of the meat as possible will be exposed to the grill. (Make more skewers if you have meat left over.) Grill at a high heat for 2–3 minutes on each side, or until the meat is thoroughly cooked through. Serve on a platter with lettuce, parsley or coriander, with the sauce on the side.

SOUPS AND **SALADS**

Although Westerners like to have soup as a separate course, in Thailand it is served with other dishes. People ladle spoonfuls of soup from a communal bowl onto the rice on their plates. There are two main categories of soup – spicy like this one and plain like the one on page 49. Tom Yam Kung is a traditional Thai soup, with an aroma created by kaffir lime leaves and lemongrass. It is definitely a must on the menu in all Thai restaurants, and easy to make at home.

hot and sour soup with prawns

tom yam kung

1.25 litres chicken stock

1 tablespoon tom yam sauce

4 kaffir lime leaves, finely chopped

2 stalks of tender lemongrass, coarsely sliced

3 tablespoons freshly squeezed lemon or lime juice

3 tablespoons Thai fish sauce

2 small fresh red or green chillies, finely sliced

2 teaspoons sugar

12 straw mushrooms, halved (canned mushrooms will do)

12 raw king prawns, peeled and deveined

serves 4

Heat the stock in a saucepan and add the tom yam sauce. Add the lime leaves, lemongrass, lemon juice, fish sauce, chillies and sugar. Bring to the boil and simmer for 2 minutes. Add the mushrooms and prawns, stir and cook for a further 2–3 minutes, or until the prawns are cooked through. Ladle into soup bowls and serve.

Note Tom yam sauce is widely available, even in some supermarkets. If you can't find it, try an Oriental market, or buy mail order from one of the sources on page 142.

This is a staple dish in the Thai diet, whenever we want to something filling to eat at unusual hours. Rice soup is to the Thai breakfast menu what cereals are in the West. Then, at the other end of the day, it continues to provide a quick source of sustenance, when late night revellers stop for a middle-of-the-night bowl of rice soup at any of the 24-hour food stalls you find in Thai cities.

chicken rice soup

khaotom gai

2 tablespoons peanut or sunflower oil

2 garlic cloves, coarsely chopped

1.25 litres chicken stock

400 g cooked rice (from about 150 g raw rice)

500 g skinless boneless chicken breasts or thighs, thinly sliced

1 teaspoon chopped preserved vegetables (tang chi)

2 tablespoons Thai fish sauce

2 tablespoons soy sauce

1 teaspoon sugar

2.5 cm fresh ginger, peeled and cut into fine shreds

½ teaspoon freshly ground white pepper

to serve

1 spring onion, finely sliced

a few fresh coriander leaves

serves 4

Heat the oil in a small frying pan, add the garlic and fry until golden brown. Set aside to infuse, reserving both the oil and the garlic.

Heat the stock in a large saucepan, add the cooked rice and slices of chicken and bring to the boil.

Stir in the preserved vegetables, fish sauce, soy sauce, sugar, ginger and white pepper and simmer gently for about 30 seconds, or until the chicken is cooked through.

Transfer to a serving bowl and trickle over a little of the reserved garlic oil. Top with finely sliced spring onion and fresh coriander leaves.

Note In Thailand, we always make this from leftover rice – we don't start from scratch. Keep leftover rice in the refrigerator and use it as soon as possible for dishes like this rice soup and for fried rice.

While Tom Yam is well known in Western countries, Tom Som is less so, although it is an equal favourite inside Thailand. However, that lack of familiarity in the West can change because the ingredients are now more widely available. The sparerib-based stock includes a mixture of garlic, shallots, ginger and tamarind water – the latter contributing its strong, sour taste. It offers an exciting alternative to the traditional Tom Yam soup.

sparerib and tamarind soup

tom som

1 teaspoon black peppercorns

1 tablespoon finely chopped coriander root

2 garlic cloves

4 small shallots

1 tablespoon peanut or sunflower oil

1.25 litres chicken stock

500 g small pork spareribs, chopped into 2.5 cm pieces

5 cm fresh ginger, finely sliced into matchsticks

2 tablespoons tamarind water

2 tablespoons sugar

3 tablespoons Thai fish sauce

4 spring onions, chopped into 2.5 cm lengths

serves 4

Using a mortar and pestle, pound the peppercorns, coriander root, garlic and shallots to form a paste.

Heat the oil in a large saucepan, add the paste and fry for 5 seconds, stirring well. Add the stock and bring to the boil, stirring well. Add the spareribs and return to the boil.

Add the ginger, tamarind water, sugar, fish sauce and spring onions. Return to the boil again and simmer for 1 minute. Ladle into a bowl and serve.

Note Preparing tamarind

If you can't find tamarind water, or the pulp in block form, tamarind paste is available in small bottles in Oriental supermarkets. For this recipe, mix 1 tablespoon paste with 1 tablespoon water.

Tamarind pulp is also available in block form. To prepare your own tamarind water, mix 1 tablespoon tamarind pulp in a bowl with 150 ml hot water, mashing with a fork. As you mix the pulp and water, the water absorbs the taste of the tamarind. When the water is cool, you can squeeze the tamarind pulp to extract more juice (and you can remove any seeds). Pour off the juice into a container and set aside for use in recipes. It will keep for about a week in the refrigerator.

This vegetarian salad looks like any Western salad. But, just like all other salads, that magical ingredient which makes it unique is the dressing. From my point of view, the dressing for this salad is as good as any in Western cuisines.

vegetable salad with peanut dressing

salad kaek

peanut or sunflower oil, for deep-frying

2 blocks of firm beancurd, about 5 cm square

125 g beansprouts, rinsed, drained and trimmed

125 g Chinese longbeans, chopped into 2.5 cm lengths

2 medium tomatoes, thinly sliced

125 g cucumber, thinly sliced

125 g white cabbage, thinly sliced, then broken into strands

2 hard-boiled eggs, shelled and quartered

peanut dressing

2 tablespoons peanut or sunflower oil

1 tablespoon Red Curry Paste (page 141)

300 ml coconut milk

½ teaspoon salt

1 tablespoon sugar

4 tablespoons crushed peanuts

serves 4

To make the dressing, heat the oil in a wok or frying pan and stir in the curry paste. Add the coconut milk and stir well. Add the salt, sugar and peanuts and stir well. Cook briefly until the coconut milk comes to the boil. Remove immediately from the heat.

To make the salad, fill a wok or saucepan about one-third full with the peanut oil and heat until a scrap of noodle will fluff up immediately. Using a slotted spoon, add the beancurd to the hot oil and deep-fry until golden. Remove with a slotted spoon, drain on kitchen paper and set aside.

Arrange all the vegetables and eggs in a salad bowl. Thinly slice the beancurd and put the slices in the bowl. Serve with the dressing, either separately, or poured over the salad and tossed.

In Thailand, yam (salad) is essential in every meal. A yam is a mixture of many different ingredients and flavours. It can include vegetables, meats, shellfish, fish and herbs and is always spicy.

seafood salad

yam talay

crisp lettuce leaves, such as baby cos or Little Gem

1 small onion, thinly sliced and separated into rings

100 g pineapple segments

100 g shelled mussels

100 g shelled baby clams

100 g peeled raw prawns, deveined and halved lengthways

100 g baby squid, chopped into small rings

100 g fish balls, halved

coriander, to serve

salad dressing

2 garlic cloves, very finely chopped

4 small red or green chillies, very finely chopped

2 tablespoons roasted peanuts, crushed

1 tablespoon sugar

3 tablespoons Thai fish sauce

3 tablespoons freshly squeezed lime juice

serves 4

To make the dressing, put the garlic, chillies, peanuts, sugar, fish sauce and lime juice in a bowl and mix well. Set aside.

To make the salad, put the lettuce leaves, onion rings and pineapple segments in a large serving bowl and set aside.

Add more water to the saucepan, bring to the boil, then add the prawns, squid and fish balls. Return to the boil for 1–2 minutes, just until the prawns are opaque. Do not overcook or the seafood will be tough. Remove immediately with a slotted spoon and put in a mixing bowl.

Rinse out the saucepan, add all the seafood and fish balls and pour over the prepared dressing. Heat and stir briefly, just long enough to reheat the seafood, no more than a minute. Spoon the seafood and dressing into the bowl of lettuce, toss well, top with coriander and serve.

Notes If using unshelled mussels and clams, you will need about 250 g of each. Heat a little water in a large saucepan, add the cleaned mussels, put the lid on tightly and shake the pan a little. After a minute or so, take off the lid and remove the open mussels to a large bowl and let cool. Discard any that won't open. When all the mussels are done, repeat with the clams. When all are cool, reserve some in their shells for serving, then take the remainder out of the shells and put in the mixing bowl.

Fish balls are kept in the refrigerator cabinet in Oriental stores. If unavailable, use extra prawns.

Papaya grows everywhere in Thailand and is freely available. Young, unripened papaya is a basic salad ingredient in street food stalls, where it is pounded with fresh, spicy ingredients into a cold dish to accompany others. Now this staple dish has found great popularity in the West as the basis of a cold salad mixed with more expensive seafood such as crab, lobster, prawns or squid.

papaya salad with squid
som tam plamuk

500 g squid, cleaned, with tentacles separated

4 garlic cloves, peeled

3–4 small fresh red or green chillies

4 Chinese long beans, chopped into 5 cm lengths

500 g fresh green papaya, peeled, deseeded and cut into fine slivers

2 tomatoes, cut into wedges

4 tablespoons Thai fish sauce

2 tablespoons sugar

4 tablespoons lime juice

to serve

a selection of fresh firm green vegetables in season, such as iceberg lettuce, cucumber or white cabbage

lime wedges

serves 4

To prepare the squid tubes, slit down both sides of the tubes and open out. Put on a board soft side up, then lightly run your knife diagonally, both ways, without cutting all the way through, making diamond patterns. The squid will then cook evenly and curl up attractively. Alternatively, just cut the tubes into slices.

Put 600 ml water in a saucepan, bring to the boil, add the squid and simmer for 3 minutes, drain and set aside.

Using a large mortar and pestle, pound the garlic to a paste, then add the chillies and pound again. Add the longbeans, breaking them up slightly. Stir in the papaya with a spoon. Lightly pound together, then stir in the tomatoes and lightly pound again. Add the squid and mix well.

Add the fish sauce, sugar and lime juice, stirring well, then transfer to a serving dish. Serve with fresh raw vegetables and lime wedges, using any leaves as a scoop for the spicy mixture.

Note If Chinese longbeans aren't available (though they are best for salads), use green beans – about 12, topped, tailed and halved.

Salads in general are perceived as lighter in the diet than most other cooked meals. In Thailand, women regard this vermicelli salad as a slimming aid.

vermicelli salad

yam wun sen

125 g minced pork

10 raw prawns, shelled, deveined and coarsely chopped

½ packet (130 g) thin rice vermicelli noodles

10 large dried black fungus mushrooms, soaked for about 10 minutes in cold water until soft, then coarsely chopped

1 large celery stalk, finely sliced

2 tablespoons Thai fish sauce

1 tablespoon sugar

3 tablespoons lime juice

about 6 small red chillies, finely chopped

about 6 spring onions, thinly sliced

coriander leaves, to serve

serves 4

Heat 3 tablespoons water in a saucepan, add the minced pork and prawns and stir well until the meat is just cooked through.

Add the noodles, mushrooms, celery, fish sauce, sugar, lime juice, chillies and spring onions.

Stir well, transfer to a serving platter and top with coriander leaves.

Notes Vermicelli are thin rice flour noodles. They are always sold dried, but are already cooked. Soak in cold water until soft, then chop coarsely.

If the dried black fungus mushrooms are very large, they may have a small hard piece in the middle, which should be cut out and discarded.

Traditionally, Asian diets did not make use of salads as we know them in the West. Over time, culinary arts and tastes have transferred across cultures, and Oriental ingredients have fused with Western salad concepts. Here, we have a very Thai-style salad in a cold dish using traditional Thai ingredients. The result is a more flavourful cold salad dish than is normally seen on Western menus.

chicken salad with mint and roasted sesame seeds
yam gai

about 10 cm cucumber
2 skinless chicken breasts
3 small celery stalks, finely sliced
3 spring onions, thickly sliced
2 tablespoons Thai fish sauce
2 tablespoons freshly squeezed lime juice
3 small red or green chillies, finely sliced
1 tablespoon finely chopped mint leaves
2 tablespoons roasted sesame seeds
2 tablespoons sesame oil

serves 4

To prepare the cucumber, cut it in half lengthways and scrape out the seeds with a teaspoon. Cut in half crossways, then cut each piece into matchsticks.

Bring a saucepan of water to the boil, add the chicken breasts and poach at a gentle simmer until cooked through. Drain and let cool.

Shred the meat into small pieces over a bowl, letting any liquid it may retain fall into the bowl. Add the cucumber, celery, spring onions, fish sauce, lime juice, chillies, mint, sesame seeds and sesame oil to the bowl and stir well. Spoon onto a plate and serve.

SNACKS AND ONE-DISH MEALS

Many Thai dishes are designed to be served with three or four others as part of a meal. Others were always single-serve dishes, such as this one, Pad Thai, which began as street food. The original recipe contained no meat but you can create your own flavour by adding your choice of meat or seafood. This has become the best-recognized Thai dish among foreigners.

thai fried noodles
gueyteow pad thai

3 tablespoons peanut or sunflower oil

2 garlic cloves, finely chopped

2 tablespoons dried shrimp

80 g ready-fried beancurd, cut into 1.25 cm cubes

2 eggs

1 packet (about 500 g) medium rice stick noodles

2 tablespoons preserved radish (chipo), finely chopped

4 spring onions, finely sliced

4 tablespoons chopped roasted peanuts

125 g beansprouts, rinsed, drained and trimmed

1 teaspoon chilli powder

1 tablespoon sugar

2 tablespoons Thai fish sauce

2 tablespoons light soy sauce

4 tablespoons freshly squeezed lemon or lime juice

a sprig of coriander, coarsely chopped

1 lemon or lime, cut into wedges, to serve

serves 2–4

Heat the oil in a wok or frying pan, add the garlic and dried shrimp and fry until golden brown. Add the ready-fried beancurd and stir briefly. Break the eggs into the wok, cook for a moment, then stir. Add the noodles, stir well, then add the preserved radish and spring onions. Add half the peanuts and half the beansprouts. Stir well, then add the chilli powder, sugar, fish sauce, soy sauce and lemon juice.

Stir well and transfer to a plate. Top with the remaining peanuts and beansprouts and the chopped coriander. Serve with lemon wedges.

Notes Thai dishes are eaten with a fork and spoon, with the fork being used to push the food onto the spoon. The exceptions are noodle dishes, which were imported from China and so are eaten with chopsticks.

Sen lek or Jantaboon noodles are flat, medium rice flour noodles, often called rice sticks. They are usually dried. Soften them in a bowl of hot water from the tap for 10 minutes, then drain and rinse in cold water.

Traditional Thai meals are sharing occasions, with several dishes being prepared and presented, usually including a mix of something salty, something sweet, something crunchy and so on. This dish is seen as sweet. In the West, it has become a stand-alone snack dish. You need patience to prepare Mee Krop – it can take quite a while to get the optimum result, but it will be well worth your time.

crispy noodles
mee krop

peanut or sunflower oil, for deep-frying

1 packet (250 g) thin rice noodles

sauce

2 tablespoons peanut or sunflower oil

125 g firm beancurd,
cut into 1 cm cubes or thin strips

60 g dried shrimp

4 garlic cloves, finely chopped

4 small shallots, finely chopped

3 tablespoons Thai fish sauce

2 tablespoons palm sugar

2 tablespoons tomato sauce

4 tablespoons freshly squeezed
lemon or lime juice

½ teaspoon chilli powder

to serve

2 tablespoons peanut or sunflower oil

1 egg, lightly beaten with
1 tablespoon cold water

60 g beansprouts, rinsed, drained and trimmed

4 spring onions, cut into 2.5 cm slivers

2 medium fresh red chillies, deseeded
and finely sliced lengthways

2 whole heads of pickled garlic,
finely sliced crossways

serves 4

Fill a wok one-third full with the oil and heat until medium hot. Add the noodles and deep-fry until golden brown and crisp. Drain and set aside. Pour the oil into a heatproof container for another use.

Pour the oil for the sauce into the wok and fry the strips of beancurd until crisp. Remove with a slotted spoon and set aside. Fry the dried shrimp until crisp. Remove with a slotted spoon and set aside.

Add the garlic to the wok, fry until golden brown, drain and set aside. Add the shallots and fry until brown. Add the fish sauce, sugar, tomato sauce and lemon juice and stir well until the mixture begins to caramelize. Add the chilli powder and the reserved beancurd and garlic and stir until they have soaked up some of the liquid. Set aside.

Using a separate pan, heat the oil for the garnish and drip in the egg mixture to make little scraps of fried egg. Drain and set aside. Return the main sauce to the heat and crumble in the crispy noodles, mixing gently and briefly. Turn on to a serving dish and sprinkle with beansprouts, spring onions, fried egg scraps, chillies and pickled garlic and serve.

Notes Sen mee are thin, dried rice flour noodles.

Pickled garlic is widely available in bottles or jars from Chinatown or South-east Asian stores, or from mail order or on-line sources (page 142).

This quick vegetarian stir-fry *mélange* is widely popular because it offers something to suit almost any taste. The curry paste provides the hot flavour and the vegetables add a wholesome crispness. While the vegetable mixture shown here represents some popular ingredients, this recipe lends itself to personal creativity, so add your favourite crunchy vegetables.

2 tablespoons peanut or sunflower oil

2 garlic cloves, finely chopped

1 tablespoon Red Curry Paste (page 141)

500 g ready-cooked egg noodles

80 g oyster mushrooms, coarsely sliced

2 small celery stalks, finely chopped

5–6 ears of baby corn, halved lengthways

80 g beansprouts, rinsed, drained and trimmed

3 spring onions, finely sliced diagonally

2 medium tomatoes, cut into wedges

3 tablespoons light soy sauce

1 teaspoon sugar

serves 4

egg noodles stir-fried with vegetables and curry paste

mee sua pad prik gaeng

Heat the oil in a wok until a light haze appears. Add the garlic, fry for about 1 minute, then add the curry paste and continue stir-frying until the garlic is golden. Add the noodles, stir well, then add mushrooms, celery, corn, beansprouts, spring onions, tomatoes, soy sauce and sugar, stirring quickly. Serve on a platter.

Note Ba me egg noodles are made from egg and wheat flour.

For most Thai, just hearing the name of this dish makes their mouths water. Usually eaten as a light lunch, it is also a favourite for a late supper. Surprisingly, it is not well known to foreigners, so if you visit Thailand, do try it at one of the all-night street food stalls.

mussel pancake
hoy tod

1 kg mussels (about 30–40), soaked, cleaned and debearded

2 tablespoons peanut or sunflower oil, plus extra if necessary

1 egg, beaten briefly with a fork

125 g beansprouts, rinsed, drained and trimmed

4 spring onions, coarsely chopped

freshly ground white pepper, to taste

2 tablespoons light soy sauce

2 tablespoons Thai fish sauce

1 teaspoon sugar

a few fresh coriander leaves, to serve

batter

3 tablespoons rice flour

3 tablespoons plain flour

a pinch of salt

1 egg

chilli-vinegar sauce

4 tablespoons rice or white wine vinegar

2 small fresh chillies, finely sliced into rings

1 teaspoon sugar

serves 4

Heat a little water in a large saucepan, add the cleaned mussels, put the lid on tightly and shake the pan until they open. Remove to a bowl as they do so, but discard any that won't open. Let the mussels cool a little, then remove them from their shells and discard the shells.

To make the chilli-vinegar sauce, put the vinegar, sliced chillies and sugar in a small bowl, mix well and set aside.

To make the batter, mix the rice flour, plain flour and salt in a bowl. Make a hollow in the centre, break in the egg and add a splash of water. Whisk well, making sure there are no lumps – the mixture should have the consistency of thick cream.

Add the shelled mussels to the batter, stir to coat thoroughly and set aside.

Heat the oil in a large wok or frying pan, add the mussel and batter mixture and tilt the pan from side to side to spread the mixture evenly over the surface. Cook the pancake for 1–2 minutes, then flip over and cook the other side briefly until it is set. Divide the pancake into 5–6 portions with a spatula and a wooden spoon. Lower the heat and pour the beaten egg into the pan. Quickly cook the pancake pieces in the egg, adding a little more oil if necessary.

Stir in the beansprouts and spring onions, then season with a sprinkling of white pepper. Add the soy sauce, fish sauce and sugar, turning the pancake pieces over quickly to absorb the liquid. Transfer to a warm serving dish and top with fresh coriander. Serve with the chilli-vinegar sauce.

This recipe is very traditional in Thailand, particularly in busy lunchtime restaurants where workers pour in, demanding their meals quickly. The chicken and vegetables are cooked in advance in one big pot, and simmered slowly to keep warm. Then they can be served by pouring over rice or noodles as the customer orders. For parties, it means that you can prepare the chicken and vegetable component in advance too, then just keep it warm, ready to serve when guests want to eat – and you can escape from the kitchen, circulate and enjoy your time with your guests.

chicken and vegetables on rice
khao nar gai

1 recipe Boiled Rice (page 11)

2 tablespoons peanut or sunflower oil

2 garlic cloves, finely chopped

500 g boneless chicken breast or thigh, cut into 2.5-cm strips

80 g bamboo shoots, finely sliced

80 g canned straw mushrooms, whole or cut in half if large

about 5 ears of baby corn, halved lengthways

½ small sweet red or green pepper, deseeded and chopped

2 tablespoons Thai fish sauce

2 teaspoons sugar

1 teaspoon dark soy sauce

1 tablespoon cornflour, mixed with 125 ml vegetable stock or cold water to make a thin paste

½ teaspoon freshly ground white pepper

4 spring onions, sliced diagonally into 2.5 cm lengths

a few fresh coriander leaves, chopped, to serve

serves 4

Put the cooked rice on a serving dish and keep it warm.

Heat the oil in a wok or frying pan, add the garlic and fry until golden brown. Add the chicken and stir-fry for a few seconds. Add the bamboo shoots, straw mushrooms, corn and sweet pepper and stir.

Stirring quickly after each addition, add the fish sauce, sugar, dark soy and 2 tablespoons water. Add more stock if the mixture becomes dry. Add the cornflour mixture and stir until thoroughly blended to make a slightly thickened sauce, adding a little more water or flour/water mixture if necessary.

Add the white pepper and chopped spring onions, stir quickly, then top with the coriander. Serve immediately with the cooked rice.

This traditional one-pot dish originates in the Muslim south of Thailand. There all the ingredients – chicken, rice, herbs, spices and stock – are put in a large pot at the same time and cooked together. The flavours from the meat and other ingredients permeate the larger volume of rice, creating a delicious and flavourful dish. It makes an ideal one-pot meal to prepare at home.

curried rice with steamed chicken and fresh pickle

khao mok gai

3 tablespoons peanut or sunflower oil

4 large garlic cloves, finely chopped

500 g fragrant Thai rice (jasmine rice, rinsed and drained

2 teaspoons curry powder

1 teaspoon salt

1 chicken, about 1.5 kg, cut up

600 ml chicken stock

fresh pickle

5 tablespoons rice vinegar

3 teaspoons sugar

½ teaspoon salt

7.5 cm piece of cucumber

4 small shallots, finely chopped

2–3 small fresh red chillies, thinly sliced

an electric rice cooker or bamboo steamer

serves 4

Heat the oil in a wok or frying pan, add the garlic and fry until golden brown. Stir in the rice, then add the curry powder and salt. Add the chicken pieces and stir well.

Either transfer the mixture to an electric rice cooker, add the stock, cover and cook for 20 minutes, or put the mixture in a heatproof bowl, add the stock and set in the top part of a steamer over boiling water and steam for 30 minutes. Turn off the heat and set aside with the lid on for about 30 minutes for the chicken to finish cooking.

While the chicken is steaming, make the pickle. Warm the vinegar, sugar and salt in a small saucepan, stirring until the sugar has dissolved. Remove from the heat. Cut the cucumber in half lengthways, scrape out the seeds with a teaspoon, then cut it in half again and slice very finely. Add to the sauce with the chopped shallots and chillies. Stir well, pour into a small bowl and serve with the steamed chicken.

Laap is an original dish from Isaan, in the north-east of Thailand, where it will often be consumed with alcoholic drinks at social gatherings. As this is a less affluent region of Thailand, local people are creative in the meats they use for this style of cooking, often using beef, buffalo, river fish, prawns, frogs and other wild animals. The dish is hot and spicy, usually with a mixture of hot chilli, garlic and other ingredients that provide salty and sharp tastes.

spicy duck with sticky rice
khao neuw-laap pet

500 g (625 ml) sticky (glutinous) rice

1 tablespoon finely chopped lemongrass

1 tablespoon finely chopped galangal or ginger

3 tablespoons Thai fish sauce

3 tablespoons freshly squeezed lime juice, about 1½ limes

2 teaspoons sugar

1 teaspoon chilli powder

4 skinless duck breasts, finely chopped

5 small shallots, thinly sliced

4 spring onions, finely chopped

20 fresh mint leaves

raw crisp green vegetables, cut into bite-sized pieces, to serve

serves 4

To make the sticky rice, put the rice in a bowl or pan, cover with water and let soak for at least 3 hours, or overnight if possible. Drain and rinse thoroughly. Line the perforated part of a steamer with a double thickness of muslin, and spread the rice over the muslin. Heat the water in the bottom of the steamer to boiling and steam the rice over moderate heat for 30 minutes.

To make the spicy duck, put the lemongrass, galangal, fish sauce, lime juice, sugar, chilli powder and 2 tablespoons water in a saucepan and heat quickly. Add the duck and mix well until the meat is cooked through. Add the shallots and spring onions and cook for a few seconds more. Then add fresh mint leaves, transfer to a serving dish and serve with a selection of raw crisp green vegetables and steamed sticky rice.

Note Galangal is widely available in markets selling South-east Asian produce. Fresh ginger is used as a common substitute in the West, though it has a totally different flavour and the recipe will not taste the same.

Khao and *pad* are perhaps the two most common and important words travellers in Thailand learn, because with these you can always get a basic yet filling dish in any restaurant. This is a staple recipe available all day in restaurants across the country. It is simple to prepare, not too hot to the taste and can be a light snack or a complete meal, depending on your portion size. While here we show only the most basic pork recipe, there are many variations found in restaurants, including versions made with chillies, seafood or chicken.

fried rice with pork and soy sauce
khao pad si-ew moo

1 recipe Boiled Rice (page 11)
2 tablespoons peanut or sunflower oil
2 garlic cloves, finely chopped
500 g lean pork, such as fillet, finely slivered
2 eggs
½ onion, coarsely sliced
60 g broccoli, cut into small florets
1 small carrot, thickly sliced
1 tablespoon dark soy sauce
1 medium tomato, cut into wedges
a pinch of sugar
2 tablespoons Thai fish sauce
2 spring onions, finely sliced
freshly ground white pepper

serves 4

First cook the rice according to the recipe on page 11. Let cool.

Heat the oil in a wok or frying pan, add the garlic and fry until golden brown. Add the pork and stir-fry briefly over high heat. Break the eggs into the pan and stir well. Add the rice and mix well. Stir in the onion, broccoli, carrot, soy sauce, tomato, sugar, fish sauce and spring onions.

Transfer to a serving dish, season with white pepper and serve.

This dish originated in China, but has been adapted to the Thai style with some local ingredients. Thailand has for centuries attracted migrants from neighbouring countries, notably China, and each ethnic group has brought diversity to the Thai culinary repertoire. This dish is based on pork barbecued in traditional Chinese style, as found in Chinese restaurants worldwide – served with rice or noodles, in soups, and as a filling in buns. Here it has a Thai flavour.

barbecued pork with rice
khao moo daeng

1 kg pork belly strips or boneless spareribs

4 tablespoons tomato purée

2 tablespoons dark soy sauce

4 tablespoons light soy sauce

4 tablespoons sugar

chilli and vinegar sauce

4 tablespoons rice vinegar

2 small fresh red chillies, cut into thin rounds

salty sauce

500 ml pork or chicken stock

2 tablespoons light soy sauce

3 tablespoons sugar

2 tablespoons Thai fish sauce

2 teaspoons rice flour mixed with 1 tablespoon water

to serve

½ cucumber, about 20 cm, thinly sliced

4 spring onions, cut into 2.5 cm lengths

a few fresh coriander leaves, coarsely chopped

2–4 hard-boiled eggs, shelled and quartered

serves 4

To prepare the pork for the barbecue, put the tomato purée, dark and light soy sauces and sugar in a large bowl. Add the pork strips and stir well to coat evenly in the sauce. Let marinate for 1 hour.

Preheat an overhead grill or barbecue. Put the marinated pork under or over the heat, turning the pieces from time to time until cooked through.

While the pork is cooking, make the sauces. To make the chilli and vinegar sauce, mix the vinegar and chilli in a small bowl and set aside.

To make the salty sauce, heat the stock in a saucepan, add the soy sauce, sugar and fish sauce and stir well. Bring to the boil and simmer for 1 minute. Sprinkle the rice flour mixture over the liquid and whisk gently until the sauce thickens.

Cut the pork into very thin slices. Put a heap of rice on each plate and top with thin slices of barbecued pork. Pour over a generous helping of the salty sauce. Add sliced cucumber, some spring onion, coriander and hard-boiled egg to each plate and serve with the chilli and vinegar sauce.

This recipe is a light, easy-to-make, quick-fry dry noodle dish. In my early schooldays, this was one of my regular lunchtime meals – it provided enough nutrition to get me through the afternoon, but could be eaten quickly enough to leave most of the lunch break free to kick a football around the school yard.

river noodles with beef and dark soy sauce
pad si yew nua

2 tablespoons peanut or sunflower oil

4 garlic cloves, finely chopped

500 g lean beef, such as fillet, finely sliced

2 eggs

1 packet (500 g) wide rice noodles

1 teaspoon finely sliced fresh ginger

250 g broccoli, thickly sliced

2 tablespoons dark soy sauce

1 teaspoon sugar

3 tablespoons Thai fish sauce

freshly ground white pepper

1 green chilli, finely shredded

serves 4

Heat the oil in a wok, add the garlic and fry until golden brown. Add the beef, stir, then cook briefly. Break the eggs into the mixture, stir, add the noodles and ginger, cook quickly, then add the broccoli and stir again.

Add the dark soy, sugar and fish sauce, stirring quickly after each addition. Stir again, transfer to a serving dish, sprinkle with white pepper, top with the shredded chilli, then serve.

Notes To make the beef easier to slice, wrap it in clingfilm and freeze for 1 hour. Unwrap and slice very finely.

Sen yai are broad, flat, rice flour noodles. If using fresh noodles, soak in hot water to separate, then boil for 1 minute. If using dried noodles, soak in a bowl of boiling water for 4 minutes, then boil for 2–3 minutes.

CURRIES
AND **PICKLES**

Salty eggs are a favourite in Thailand. Traditionally, we prefer duck eggs, because they are considered firmer when hard-boiled. If you can't find duck eggs, use large chicken eggs instead. The eggs can be eaten simply on their own, or served with rice, salad or crunchy Chinese longbeans. To make the salty eggs, you have to start three weeks ahead, but if you have access to a good Oriental market, you should be able to buy them already prepared.

spicy longbeans with salty eggs
pad prik king kai-kem

peanut or sunflower oil, for deep-frying, plus 2 tablespoons extra

180 g ready-fried beancurd, finely sliced

2 teaspoons finely chopped garlic

1 tablespoon Red Curry Paste (page 141)

250 g Chinese longbeans, chopped into 2.5 cm lengths

2 tablespoons light soy sauce

4 tablespoons vegetable stock

1 teaspoon sugar

1 tablespoon ground roasted peanuts

4 kaffir lime leaves, finely chopped

salty eggs

8 eggs (duck eggs are preferred, but large chicken eggs are quite satisfactory)

300 g salt

serves 4

(V)

To prepare the salty eggs, put the eggs in a preserving jar, being careful not to crack the shells. Put the salt and 750 ml water in a saucepan and heat until the salt has dissolved. Let cool, then pour the mixture over the eggs in the jar. Seal the jar and leave for 3 weeks, after which the eggs can be boiled or fried. To use them in this dish, you will need 2 hard-boiled eggs (see note). Cut the eggs in half with the shells still on, then scoop out the halves with a teaspoon. Cut each half in half again and set aside.

Fill a wok one-third full with the peanut oil and heat until a piece of noodle will fluff up immediately. Add the beancurd and deep-fry until the white sides are golden brown. Remove with a slotted spoon, drain and set aside.

Heat the 2 tablespoons of oil in a wok or frying pan, add the garlic and fry until golden brown. Stir in the red curry paste. Add the longbeans, soy sauce, stock, sugar, peanuts, lime leaves and fried beancurd. Stir-fry until the beans are done to your taste (I like them very crisp). Serve on a platter with the salty eggs.

Notes Though you could make this dish with regular green beans, Chinese longbeans are very good in cold or cool dishes. They have more bite and crunch than regular beans. Find them in Chinese and South-east Asian markets and sometimes in larger supermarkets.

For hard-boiled salty eggs, boil 5–6 minutes for hen eggs or 6–8 minutes for duck eggs. Alternatively, put the eggs in cold water, bring to the boil, turn off the heat and let cool.

Curry originated in the Indian subcontinent and migrated eastwards long before it travelled west to Europe and North America. Over centuries, it has been adapted to local ingredients and tastes in several other Asian countries, notably Thailand, where it is generally considered that many of our curries are even hotter and more flavourful than their Indian cousins. Red curry paste is used as the core curry ingredient in many Thai dishes.

2 tablespoons peanut or sunflower oil

2 tablespoons Red Curry Paste (page 141)

600 ml coconut cream

600 ml vegetable stock

4 Chinese longbeans, cut into 2.5 cm pieces

4 carrots, cut into matchsticks

5 ears of baby corn, cut into 2.5 cm pieces

80 g cauliflower, cut into florets

4 kaffir lime leaves, coarsely chopped

2 large fresh red or green chillies, coarsely sliced

3 tablespoons light soy sauce

2 teaspoons sugar

½ teaspoon salt

6 small round green aubergines, quartered

30 fresh basil leaves

serves 4

vegetable curry
gaeng ped pak

Put the oil in a saucepan, heat well, then quickly stir in the curry paste. Add the coconut cream, mixing well. Add the vegetable stock and stir briefly.

Add the longbeans, carrots, corn, cauliflower, lime leaves, chillies, soy sauce, sugar, salt and aubergines. Stir well, then cook for a few minutes until the vegetables are cooked to your taste (I like them crisp but tender).

Add the basil leaves, stir once, then ladle into a bowl and serve with other Thai curries and rice.

Green curry is my mother's speciality, so this is a staple dish from my childhood. With more than 20 years' experience in the food industry and being a head chef myself, I can confidently say that I have never tasted a green curry as good as my mother's.

green curry with prawns

gaeng keow-wan gung

2 tablespoons peanut or sunflower oil

2 garlic cloves, finely chopped

2 tablespoons Green Curry Paste (page 141)

12 raw king prawns, shelled and deveined

600 ml coconut cream

600 ml vegetable stock

2 large fresh red chillies, sliced diagonally into thin ovals

4 tablespoons Thai fish sauce

8 round green Thai aubergines, quartered, or 1 Chinese eggplant, cut into ½-inch slices

1 tablespoon sugar

30 fresh sweet basil leaves

serves 4

Heat the oil in a large saucepan, add the garlic and fry until golden brown. Stir in the curry paste, mixing well. Add the prawns and stir-fry until just cooked through. Add the coconut cream and bring to the boil, stirring constantly. Add the stock. Return to the boil, stirring constantly.

Keeping the curry simmering, add the chillies, fish sauce, aubergines and sugar and simmer until the aubergines are cooked but still crunchy (do not overcook or the prawns will be tough).

Stir in the basil leaves just before pouring into the serving bowl. Serve with rice and other Thai dishes.

In this quick, pan-fried curry, the flavour comes mainly from chilli oil. As soon as the pan and oil are heated, add the clams, steam for just a few minutes and they're cooked.

baby clams with chilli oil and holy basil

hoy pad nam prik pow

1 tablespoon peanut or sunflower oil

2 garlic cloves, finely chopped

1 tablespoon chilli oil (see below)

1 kg baby clams, in the shell

2 tablespoons Thai fish sauce

2 small red chillies, finely sliced

20 leaves holy basil

chilli oil (nam prik pow)

2 tablespoons peanut or sunflower oil

4 tablespoons finely chopped garlic

4 tablespoons finely chopped shallots

4 tablespoons finely chopped dried red chillies

½ teaspoon salt

1 tablespoon sugar

serves 4

To make the chilli oil, heat the oil in a wok, add the garlic and stir-fry until golden brown. Remove the garlic with a fine sieve and set aside. Add the shallots to the wok and stir-fry until brown and crispy. Remove with a sieve and set aside. Add the chillies to the wok and stir-fry until they begin to darken. Remove with a sieve.

Using a mortar and pestle, pound the chillies, garlic and shallots together. Put the mixture back in the wok and stir over low heat. Stir in the salt and sugar and mix to make a thick, slightly oily reddish black sauce, not a paste. Use 1 tablespoon for this recipe and reserve the rest for another use.

Heat the oil in a large frying pan, add the garlic and fry until golden brown. Add 1 tablespoon of the chilli oil and the baby clams and stir thoroughly. Add the fish sauce, chillies, and 4 tablespoons water. Stir thoroughly, add the basil, cover the pan and let steam for a few minutes until the clams have opened. Discard any that don't open. Stir again, transfer to a warmed dish and serve.

Paenang curries differ from most other Thai dishes in being rather dry – normally, they are very wet, with accompanying sauces, similar to many Indian curries. While it is not clear how this curry entered our cuisine, it is thought, judging from the name, that it may have originated in the far south of Thailand, near Malaysia (Penang is in Malaysia).

chicken panaeng curry
panaeng gai

600 ml coconut cream
2 tablespoons peanut or sunflower oil
2 garlic cloves, finely chopped
2 tablespoons Panaeng Curry Paste (page 141)
500 g boneless chicken breast, thinly sliced
3 tablespoons Thai fish sauce
2 teaspoons sugar
4 kaffir lime leaves, finely chopped
20 holy basil leaves
2 long red chillies, slivered

serves 4

Gently heat the coconut cream in a small saucepan, but do not let it boil. Set aside. Reserve 1 tablespoon for serving.

Heat the oil in a wok or frying pan until a light haze appears, add the garlic and fry until golden brown. Add the curry paste and stir-fry for a few seconds. Add the chicken and stir-fry until it is lightly cooked. Add the coconut cream, stir well, then add the fish sauce and sugar, stir well. Just before serving, stir in the lime leaves, holy basil and some of the slivered chillies. Spoon into a bowl and top with the reserved 1 tablespoon coconut cream and the remaining chillies.

A real fusion of Chinese (noodles) and Indian (curry), prepared in a particularly Thai way, this dish adds to the variety and excitement of Thai cuisine. It could well originate further south, around the Straits of Malacca, where the Nonya peoples, a mixture of Chinese and Malay, developed many dishes that crossed the boundaries between Chinese and Muslim diets and culinary styles.

chicken curry noodle
gueyteow gaeng

½ packet (250 g) dried medium rice noodles
500 g chicken, cut into 2.5 cm cubes
2 hard-boiled eggs
2 tablespoons peanut or sunflower oil
1 block prepared fried beancurd, finely sliced
4 pink Thai shallots or 2 regular ones, finely sliced
4 garlic cloves, finely chopped
1 tablespoon Red Curry Paste (page 141)
600 ml coconut cream
1 teaspoon curry powder
4 tablespoons Thai fish sauce
2 teaspoons sugar
2 tablespoons ground roasted peanuts
coriander leaves, to serve

serves 4

Soak, rinse and drain the noodles. Put the chicken in a small pan and cover with water. Simmer gently for 10–15 minutes, then remove from the heat and set aside, reserving the cooking water. Cut the eggs into quarters and set aside.

Heat the oil in a wok or frying pan, add the sliced beancurd and fry until slightly crisp; drain, and set aside. Reheat the oil and fry the shallots until dark golden brown and crisp. Set aside in the pan. Add the garlic and fry for a few seconds until golden brown. Stir in the curry paste and cook for a few seconds. Add the coconut cream, stir thoroughly and heat through for another few seconds.

Using a slotted spoon or strainer, remove the chicken from its pan and add to the mixture. Stir to make sure each piece is covered with the curry. Add 500 ml of the water in which the chicken has been cooked (make up the amount with cold water if necessary), then add the curry powder, fish sauce and sugar. Stir well and cook for about 5 minutes.

Have serving bowls ready. Bring a saucepan of water to the boil, put the noodles in a sieve or strainer with a handle and dip into the water for 2–3 seconds to warm through. Drain and divide between the serving bowls. Arrange the quartered egg on top of the noodles. Add the peanuts to the chicken curry soup, stir and pour over the noodles. Top with the fried beancurd, fried shallots with a little of their oil, and the coriander.

Note Sen lek or Jantaboon noodles are flat, medium rice flour noodles, often called rice sticks. They are usually dried. Soften them in a bowl of hot water for 10 minutes, then drain and rinse in cold water.

The long white radish – mooli or daikon – is popular in Chinese cooking, but has also been adopted extensively in Thailand, especially in its preserved form. It particularly helps in recipes where you want a salty taste, and also adds a crunchy texture. You can buy preserved radish in Oriental markets, but if you would like to try preserving them yourself, it is very easy.

pork with fried preserved radish
pad chipo

2 tablespoons peanut or sunflower oil

2 teaspoons finely chopped garlic

250 g loin of pork, finely sliced

2 eggs

60 g preserved radish
(store-bought or homemade – see note),
sliced diagonally 5 mm thick

3 medium spring onions,
finely chopped into rings

2 tablespoons light soy sauce

2 tablespoons Thai fish sauce

1 teaspoon sugar

½ teaspoon freshly ground white pepper

coriander leaves, to serve

preserved white radish (chipo)

500 g white radish, peeled and cut in half
lengthways, then into matchsticks

250 g sugar

250 ml rice vinegar

2 tablespoons salt

serves 4

If you are making your own preserved white radish, put the pieces of radish in a bowl, sprinkle with salt and leave overnight. Next day, rinse the pieces thoroughly at least twice in cold water.

Arrange the pieces of radish in a preserving jar and set aside. Put the sugar and vinegar in a saucepan and bring to the boil. Remove from the heat and let cool. When cold, pour the mixture over the radish. Close the jar firmly and leave for 1 week.

After 1 week, remove the radish and spread on a rack to dry in the open air. In Thailand we leave them to sun-dry, which takes about 24 hours.

To make the fried pork, heat the oil in a wok, add the garlic and fry until golden brown. Add the pork, stir and cook until the meat is slightly opaque. Break the eggs into the pan, spreading the broken yolks a little. Before the egg sets, add the preserved radish and spring onion and stir rapidly. Add the soy sauce, fish sauce, sugar and white pepper, stirring rapidly. Transfer to a platter, top with coriander leaves and serve.

Note There are two kinds of preserved radish – sweet or salty. The one used in this recipe is the sweet kind. If you have the salty kind, soak in cold water for 5–10 minutes, then drain and squeeze out the water before proceeding with the recipe.

In the north of Thailand, they have adapted the traditional curry taste to get a sweet and sour flavour, common to other non-curry Thai dishes. This is achieved by using pickled garlic to provide a blend of sweet and sour tastes. In the north, this dish would be eaten with plain sticky rice.

pork curry with pickled garlic
gaeng hung lay

2 tablespoons peanut or sunflower oil

2 garlic cloves, finely chopped

2 tablespoons Red Curry Paste (page 141)

500 g boneless pork with a little fat, finely slivered

600 ml coconut cream

5 cm fresh ginger, peeled and finely chopped

5 tablespoons chicken stock or water

3 tablespoons Thai fish sauce

2 teaspoons sugar

½ teaspoon ground turmeric

2 teaspoons freshly squeezed lemon or lime juice

4 whole heads of pickled garlic, finely sliced crossways

serves 4

Heat the oil in a wok or frying pan, add the garlic and fry until golden brown. Add the curry paste and stir well. Add the pork and stir-fry over high heat until cooked through, approximately 5 minutes.

Pour in the coconut cream and stir until the liquid begins to reduce and thicken. Do not boil. Add the ginger, chicken stock, fish sauce, sugar, turmeric, lemon juice and pickled garlic, stirring constantly.

Transfer to a serving bowl and serve.

Note Pickled garlic is widely available in bottles or jars from Chinatown or South-east Asian stores, or from mail order or on-line sources (page 142).

If you like a milder curry, this is the dish for you. It originates in the Muslim south of Thailand, where people prefer less spicy foods in general. It also shows an Indian influence in the use of potatoes and nuts as key ingredients. While lamb is not part of the traditional Thai diet, this dish could be made with either lamb or chicken if you prefer.

massaman beef curry

massaman nua

600 ml coconut cream

2 tablespoons peanut or sunflower oil

2 garlic cloves, finely chopped

2 tablespoons Massaman Curry Paste (page 141)

500 g lean beef, cut into 2.5 cm cubes

3 tablespoons freshly squeezed lemon or lime juice

2 teaspoons sugar

3 tablespoons Thai fish sauce

600 ml beef stock or water

4 small potatoes, quartered

3 tablespoons whole roasted peanuts

4 pink Thai shallots or 2 regular ones, quartered

sprigs of coriander, to serve

serves 4

Gently warm the coconut cream in a small saucepan until it just starts to separate. Remove from the heat and set aside.

Heat the oil in a wok or frying pan, add the garlic and fry until golden brown. Add the curry paste, mix well and cook for a few seconds. Add half the warmed coconut cream and cook for 2–3 seconds, stirring all the time, until the mixture bubbles and starts to reduce.

Add the beef and stir it into the sauce to make sure that each piece is thoroughly coated. Stirring after each addition, add the lemon juice, sugar, fish sauce, stock and the remainder of the warmed coconut cream. Simmer gently for 15 minutes, stirring from time to time.

Add the quartered potatoes and simmer for a further 5 minutes. Add the peanuts and cook for 5 minutes more. Stir in the shallots and cook for 5 more minutes, then pour into a serving dish and top with fresh coriander. Serve with fragrant Thai rice (jasmine rice) and other dishes, such as a soup, a stir-fry, a spicy salad and fresh pickle (page 72).

I developed this modern Thai recipe to meet the growing demand for dishes that combine the best of culinary cultures across the region. Like so many Thai, my family has a mixed heritage of Chinese and Thai, so some of our recipes have developed to reflect this combination. In South-east Asia, all noodle recipes are of Chinese origin and so are usually eaten with chopsticks.

stir-fried beef noodles with curry paste
ba mee pad prik gaeng

2 tablespoons peanut or sunflower oil

4 small garlic cloves, finely chopped

1 tablespoon Green Curry Paste (page 141)

500 g beef, thinly sliced

4 nests of egg noodles

1 tablespoon dark soy sauce

3 tablespoons Thai fish sauce

2 teaspoons sugar

100 g beansprouts, rinsed, drained and trimmed

100 g broccoli, cut into small pieces, about 2.5cm

1 carrot, cut into fine matchsticks

coriander leaves, to serve

serves 4

Heat the oil in a wok or frying pan, add the garlic and fry until golden brown. Add the curry paste and stir well.

Stirring once after each addition, add the beef, drained noodles, soy sauce, fish sauce, sugar, beansprouts, broccoli and carrot.

Mix well, transfer to a serving bowl or plate and top with torn coriander.

Note Ba mee are egg and wheat flour noodles, and always sold fresh. Rinse them in warm water, boil for 3–4 minutes, then drain.

MAIN DISHES

Ever popular in my own restaurants, this is a dish I can always recommend to people new to the tastes of Thai food. They enjoy the combination of fresh prawns with the strongly aromatic flavour of basil. It's easy to vary the amount of chilli, too, in case very spicy food isn't to your taste. This is an excellent dish for the beginner cook.

prawns with chilli and basil
kung pad prik krapow

2 tablespoons peanut or sunflower oil

2 garlic cloves, finely chopped

2 small fresh red or green chillies, finely chopped

12 raw king prawns, shelled and deveined

2 medium onions, halved and thickly sliced

3 tablespoons Thai fish sauce

2 tablespoons light soy sauce

1 teaspoon sugar

30 fresh holy basil leaves

serves 4

Heat the oil in a wok or frying pan, add the garlic and chillies and fry, stirring well, until the garlic begins to brown. Stir in the prawns, then add the onions, fish sauce, soy sauce, sugar and basil, mixing well. Cook until the prawns are cooked through (it will take just a few minutes – they will become opaque). Transfer to a dish and serve with other Thai dishes, including rice.

Variations *Pad prik krapow* means 'stir-fried with basil and chilli'. You can vary this dish and, instead of prawns, use 500 g of pork, beef or chicken, all finely chopped or minced. In Thailand, the prawns would also be chopped or minced, but in the West, whole prawns are used instead.

The sweet and sour topping from this dish can be adapted to suit vegetarians. Instead of fish sauce, use extra soy sauce, then serve with rice and other vegetarian dishes.

sweet and sour fish

pad preow wan pla

1 sea bass, about 1 kg

peanut or sunflower oil, for frying

sweet and sour topping

2 teaspoons cornflour

2 tablespoons peanut or sunflower oil

2 garlic cloves, finely chopped

100 g pineapple chunks, fresh or canned

about 8 cm cucumber, quartered lengthways, then thickly sliced crossways

1 small onion, halved, then sliced into thin segments

2 small tomatoes, quartered

3 medium spring onions, coarsely chopped into 2.5 cm lengths

2 large fresh red chillies, sliced diagonally

2 tablespoons Thai fish sauce

1 tablespoon light soy sauce

1 teaspoon sugar

½ teaspoon freshly ground white pepper

electric deep-fryer or wok

serves 4

Make a diagonal cut in each side of the fish.

Fill a wok or deep-fryer one-third full with the oil or to the manufacturer's recommended level. Heat until a scrap of noodle will puff up immediately.

Add the fish and fry until golden and crispy. Remove from the oil, drain and put on a serving dish.

Mix the cornflour with 5 tablespoons water in a small cup and set aside.

Heat the oil in a wok or frying pan, add the garlic and fry until golden brown. Stirring constantly, add the pineapple, cucumber, onion, tomatoes, spring onions, chillies, fish sauce, soy sauce, sugar and pepper.

Stir the cornflour mixture to loosen it, then add to the vegetables and stir briefly to thicken the sauce. Pour over the fish, then serve.

Though the pineapple is a Thai addition, this simple chicken stir-fry originated in China. Thai pineapples are wonderfully sweet, and the sweet-and-spicy combination is typical in South-east Asian cuisines.

chicken stir-fried with ginger and pineapple
gai pad king sapparot

6 large dried black fungus mushrooms

2 tablespoons peanut or sunflower oil

2 garlic cloves, finely chopped

250 g boneless chicken, finely sliced

250 g pineapple chunks, fresh or canned

5 cm fresh ginger, peeled and cut into fine matchsticks

2 tablespoons light soy sauce

2 tablespoons Thai fish sauce

4 spring onions, chopped into 2.5 cm pieces

2 long fresh red chillies, cut diagonally into fine ovals

1 teaspoon sugar

freshly ground black pepper, to taste

serves 4

Soak the mushrooms in cold water for 10 minutes, then drain and set aside. If large, cut them into smaller pieces, discarding any hard parts.

Heat the oil in a wok or frying pan, add the garlic and fry until golden brown. Add the chicken and stir well. Stirring constantly, add the mushrooms, pineapple, ginger, soy sauce, fish sauce, spring onions, chillies, sugar and pepper. As soon as the pepper is stirred in, transfer to a dish and serve.

This dish is a combination of Thai and Chinese cuisines. Duck is not a traditional ingredient in Thai cooking, so when it does appear it is often cooked using roast duck prepared in the Chinese style. For this recipe, the key ingredient is the tamarind water. Prepare it as described on page 49.

grilled duck with tamarind sauce
ped makham

4 duck breasts, with or without skin

3 tablespoons Thai fish sauce

2 large red chillies, cut into small strips

coriander leaves, to serve

duck marinade

4 garlic cloves, finely chopped

1 tablespoon finely chopped coriander root

1 teaspoon ground cumin

2 tablespoons Thai fish sauce

1 tablespoon light soy sauce

2 teaspoons sugar

tamarind sauce

2 tablespoons peanut or sunflower oil

2 large garlic cloves, finely chopped

1 tablespoon grated fresh ginger

2 tablespoons tamarind water (page 49)

2 tablespoons vegetable stock or water

2 tablespoons sugar

serves 4

To make the marinade, put the garlic, coriander root, cumin, fish sauce, soy sauce and sugar in a bowl and mix well. Add the duck, coating it well with the mixture, and leave to marinate for 1 hour.

When ready to cook, remove the duck from the marinade and pat it dry with kitchen paper. Preheat the grill to a high heat and cook the duck for 5 minutes on each side, then slice diagonally and set aside.

To make the tamarind sauce, heat the oil in a wok or frying pan, add the garlic and fry until golden. Add the ginger, tamarind water, stock and sugar, stirring well. Add the sliced duck and sprinkle with fish sauce and strips of chilli, stirring well. Transfer to a serving dish, top with coriander and serve.

Common in farming areas, this recipe comes from the north, where whole families work in the fields from dawn to dusk. The wife will prepare the dish and take it to the fields, where it will be eaten with sticky rice – often cold – for lunch and throughout the day. Back at home in the evening, if there is some left over, it will be served for dinner too. You can also serve it as a sauce with raw or blanched vegetables, crispy pork crackling (see note below) or prawn crackers.

pork and chilli sauce

nam prik ong

2 tablespoons peanut or sunflower oil

3 garlic cloves, finely chopped

1 tablespoon Red Curry Paste (page 141)

250 g minced pork

2 large tomatoes, finely chopped

2 tablespoons Thai fish sauce

2 tablespoons freshly squeezed lemon or lime juice

1 teaspoon sugar

to serve (optional)

prawn crackers

Thai pork crackling

salad leaves

sliced shallots or other vegetables

steamed rice

serves 4

Heat the oil in a wok or frying pan until a light haze appears. Add the garlic and stir-fry until golden brown. Stir in the curry paste and stir-fry briefly.

Add the pork and stir-fry until the meat loses its pinkness. Add the tomatoes, stir, cook for 5 seconds, then add the fish sauce, lemon juice and sugar. Stir-fry for 2 minutes until the flavours are thoroughly blended.

Serve in a small bowl with your choice of prawn crackers, Thai pork crackling, salad leaves or other vegetables, or rice.

Note Thai pork crackling can be found in Oriental stores. Chinese markets might call it by its Cantonese name *ji pay*, while in Mandarin it is known as *zhu pi*.

An easy dish to prepare and cook, this is a suitable recipe for those new to Thai cooking. The combination of garlic and chilli ensures a very hot and traditional Thai flavour.

pork with garlic and fresh chilli
moo tod kratiam prik sod

2 tablespoons peanut or sunflower oil

3 large garlic cloves, finely chopped

500 g lean pork, finely sliced

2 tablespoons Thai fish sauce

2 tablespoons light soy sauce

2 large fresh red chillies, finely sliced

serves 4

Heat the oil in a wok or frying pan until a light haze appears. Add the garlic and stir-fry until golden brown. Add the pork and and stir-fry briefly.

Add the fish sauce, soy sauce and chillies, stirring briefly all the time. By now the pork should be cooked through. Spoon onto a serving dish and top with sliced spring onions. Serve with 3–4 other Thai dishes, including rice, noodles and perhaps fresh pickle.

Variations Instead of the pork, use a similar quantity of finely sliced chicken or beef, or shelled and deveined prawns.

Prawns or squid with garlic and peppercorns is another favourite Thai dish, both in Thailand and in Thai restaurants worldwide. Follow the main recipe, but instead of the chillies, use 1 teaspoon white peppercorns, crushed with a mortar and pestle.

My Aunt Chinda is a wonderful Thai cook in her own right. She greatly influenced me, both in the actual cooking of traditional Thai food, and subsequently in the business of running and managing restaurants, because she has owned and run restaurants in several of the major cities of Thailand. This recipe is one of her favourites.

stir-fried beef with aubergines and bean sauce

nua pad makua tow jiew

2 tablespoons peanut or sunflower oil

2 garlic cloves, finely chopped

4 small fresh red or green chillies, finely chopped

250 g boneless tender beef, sliced into thin slivers

1 long Thai aubergine (like Chinese or Japanese), thickly sliced or 1 long green aubergine, thickly sliced

2 tablespoons bean sauce, yellow or black

1 tablespoon light soy sauce

1 teaspoon sugar

20 sweet basil leaves

steamed rice, to serve

serves 4

Heat the oil in a wok or frying pan, add the garlic and fry until golden brown. Add the chillies and stir well. Add the beef, stir, then add the aubergine. Stir again, add the bean sauce, soy sauce and sugar, then stir-fry until the aubergine is just cooked through (cover with a lid – the steam will help it cook faster).

Add the basil leaves, stir thoroughly, then spoon onto a dish and serve with steamed rice.

Agriculture is Thailand's main industry. The farmers prepare a day's food in the morning to take into the fields for lunch and snacks. Their diets are very simple, usually quite high in carbohydrates rather than protein, as energy is the key to a hard day's work. This recipe is found mainly in the Central Regions, and would be served as a side dish with rice and other dishes.

fish and spicy sauce
nam prik pla yang

1 medium mackerel, about 500 g

1 medium onion, finely chopped

5 garlic cloves, peeled

4 large fresh red chillies, coarsely chopped

3 tablespoons Thai fish sauce

3 tablespoons lemon or lime juice

1 tablespoon coriander leaves, finely chopped

to serve

your choice of salads, lettuce, sliced radishes, celery, carrot and cucumber

kitchen foil

serves 4

Wrap the fish in foil leaving the top open and set under a preheated grill until it is thoroughly cooked through. Remove to a plate and let cool. When cool, break up the fish with your fingers to make small pieces. Discard any bones and set the flesh aside.

Wrap the onion, garlic and chillies in foil, again leaving the top open and set them under the grill. Cook until they begin to soften.

Using a large mortar and pestle, pound the onion, garlic and chillies to form a liquid paste. Stir in the fish sauce and lemon juice, then fold in the fish (see note). Spoon into a small bowl and sprinkle with coriander. Serve surrounded by a selection of salads, crisp lettuce, radish, celery, carrot and cucumber.

Note In Thailand, the fish would be mashed to a paste before folding into the mixture.

SWEET THINGS

Thailand is a country that is rich in fruits and vegetables, and they are generally high quality, as demonstrated by the volume of exports to other nations. Fruit is not just served at the end of a meal – it also appears in main meals, especially in spicy curries, stir-fries, dips and salads. In curries, you find pineapples and lychees. Salads are made with rose apples, guavas, pomelos, green mangoes or green papaya. Mangoes are also used in spicy dips and lychees as a filling in deep-fried spring rolls. A popular street food snack is green fruit sprinkled with salt and chilli. You can blend any combination of tropical fruits into a colourful and juicy salad that will sparkle like a bowl of gems on the table.

thai fruit salad

1 small ripe papaya
½ pineapple
1 ripe mango
4 rose apples (optional) or regular apples
1 ripe guava
1 tablespoon freshly squeezed lemon or lime juice
1 tablespoon sugar
10 mint leaves, finely chopped, to serve

serves 4

Peel, halve and deseed the papaya. Cut the flesh into small cubes.

Peel, core, and cube the pineapple.

Cut the cheeks off the mango, cut the flesh in diamond shapes down to the skin, turn the cheeks inside out, then scoop off the pieces with a fork.

To prepare the rose apples, cut them in half, cut out the cores and cut the flesh into small cubes.

Cut the guava in half, scoop out and discard the seeds, then cut the flesh into small cubes.

Arrange the fruit in a bowl. Add the lemon juice, sugar and chopped mint. Mix well and chill in the refrigerator before serving.

While all Thai fruits are suitable for making mouth-watering and cleansing sorbets, perhaps the star in our collection is lychee sorbet. If you cannot find fresh lychees in your neighbourhood (they are best in autumn), this recipe is also good with canned lychees.

lychee sorbet

150 g sugar

500 g fresh lychees, peeled, deseeded and finely chopped, or about 450 g canned lychees, drained and chopped

a few fresh lychees, to serve (optional)

an electric ice cream maker (optional)

serves 4

To make a sugar syrup, put the sugar in a saucepan with 300 ml water. Bring to the boil and stir until the sugar dissolves. Let cool.

Put the lychees in a blender, add the cooled syrup and blend until smooth. Freeze for about 1 hour until the mixture is slushy and frozen around the edges. Remove from the freezer, transfer to the blender, blend again, then return the mixture to the freezer for about 30 minutes.

Alternatively, if you have an electric ice cream maker, churn until the mixture is completely frozen. Transfer to a freezer-proof container and freeze until ready to serve.

Before serving, let soften in the refrigerator for about 20 minutes, then serve in scoops with a few fresh lychees, if available.

Notes This recipe is suitable for many fruits. In particular, try papaya, pineapple, kiwifruit and mango.

Make extra sugar syrup, then decant into a storage bottle and keep in the refrigerator for use in drinks and puddings. It is a very useful ingredient.

Thai puddings in general can be time consuming to prepare. While other recipes might be more popular within Thailand, for Thai living abroad, this recipe offers a time-saving treat, with ingredients commonly available. If you are new to Thai cuisine, this will be a quick and easy starting point in preparing Thai sweet dishes. Palm sugar, produced from the sap of the coconut palm, has a deep caramel flavour. It is sold in cans or compressed cakes – it should be soft brown, with a distinctive toffee-like aroma. The cakes will keep well in a sealed jar. You will find palm sugar in Oriental stores or by mail order (page 142).

sweet potatoes with palm sugar and coconut milk

man gaeng buad

500 g sweet potatoes, peeled and coarsely cut 2.5 cm cubes

1 teaspoon salt

600 ml coconut cream

5 tablespoons palm sugar

serves 4

Put the sweet potato cubes in a bowl of cold water, add the salt and let soak for 30 minutes. Drain.

Heat the coconut cream in a saucepan, add the sweet potato cubes and bring to the boil. Add the palm sugar and stir until it dissolves. Stir in 300 ml water. Return to the boil and simmer until the sweet potato is tender. Remove from the heat and serve warm.

Sago pearls are one of the most surprising and delicious additions to a sweet dish you can think of. If you have bad memories of school dinners which included sago or tapioca pudding, this will be a revelation! Sago is made from the heart of the sago palm, while tapioca is made from the root of a tropical plant called cassava or manioc. You will find both items sold under both names in Asian stores – either will do. Often, it is only the size of the pearl which is different. In this dish, they are used in a cold refreshing pudding served with crushed ice which brings out the scent of the melon and coconut milk. Sweet and revitalizing.

melon and coconut milk with sago

sa-koo taeng

6 tablespoons sago

400 ml coconut milk

6 tablespoons sugar

1 ripe melon, preferably cantaloupe, cut into 1 cm cubes

crushed ice (optional)

serves 4

Wash the sago in cold water and drain.

Pour 600 ml water into a saucepan and bring to the boil. Add the sago and return to the boil. When the sago floats to the surface (at least 15 minutes), it is cooked. Remove with a slotted spoon as it rises and transfer to a bowl of cold water.

When all the sago has been transferred, remove from the cold water and drain. Spoon into a serving bowl and set aside.

Heat the coconut milk in a saucepan. Stir in the sugar and 600 ml water, bring gently to the boil, then remove from the heat and let cool.

When cool, pour into a bowl, add the sago and melon and serve with crushed ice. If you do not have crushed ice, chill the mixture in the refrigerator before serving.

If the body could survive on fruit alone, then maybe Thailand would be the country for fruit lovers to live in. Fruits grow in abundance all year and are of excellent quality, freshness and value. Some of the fruits are very specific to regions and may not even make it to the markets of Bangkok. A great variety of these fruits are used in drinks, including bananas, guavas, papaya, oranges, pineapples, watermelon, coconuts, longans, pomelos, rambutans and mangoes. You can try this recipe with any of these fruit, and also with temperate zone fruit such as apples and pears.

tropical fruit drinks

nam-pun

1 ripe pineapple, peeled, cored and cut into small slices

ice cubes

sugar syrup (page 126)

a pinch of salt

a blender

Serves 1

Put a few slices of pineapple in a blender with ice cubes, syrup and a pinch of salt to taste (salt will bring out the flavour of the fruit). Blend well, then pour into glasses.

The variations shown here are made with papaya and guavas.

thai tea

nam cha

Tea originated in China, and moved through to Thailand over the centuries, brought by Chinese immigrants. Now many varieties are grown in the cooler, wetter hill districts of northern Thailand, which have the most suitable climate for tea. Thailand consumes many varieties of tea, and in many formats, from traditional Chinese tea, drunk plain and without sugar, to the iced teas popular in other countries, and the British style with milk and sugar. Whatever your taste in tea you should find a variety you will like here.

Thai leaf tea
sugar, to taste
ice
sweetened condensed milk

Hot tea *Cha ron*
Brew a pot of Thai tea and serve to your taste.

Iced tea without milk *Cha dum yen*
Brew a pot of Thai tea, add sugar and stir well. Let cool to room temperature, then pour over a full glass of ice.

Iced tea with milk *Cha yen*
Brew a pot of very strong hot tea. For each person, add 1 teaspoon sweetened condensed milk and sugar to taste. Let cool, then serve with a full glass of ice.

thai coffee

ka fae

Coffee, like tea, is being grown now in the Hill Tribes' areas of the north, in a project sponsored by King Rama IX. It is encouraged as an alternative to opium (banned as a cash crop in Thailand), but which is a centuries-old traditional crop of the Hill Tribes of Thailand, Burma and neighbouring countries. In the future, perhaps Thai coffee will find a niche in world markets, but in the meantime, readers may like to sample the local coffee when travelling in Thailand.

freshly ground coffee, Thai if possible
sugar, to taste
ice
sweetened condensed milk
unsweetened condensed milk

Hot coffee *Ka fae ron*
Brew a pot of filtered coffee, using your favourite blend or authentic Thai coffee if available.

Sweet iced black coffee *Oliang*
Brew strong black coffee, add sugar to taste and stir well. Let cool, then serve over ice.

Iced coffee with milk *Ka fae yen*
Brew strong black coffee, then for each person add 1 teaspoon sweetened condensed milk and sugar to taste. Stir well. Let cool to room temperature and pour the coffee over a full glass of ice. Top with unsweetened condensed milk.

CURRY PASTES

When making curry pastes, the quantities needed to make a single curry are too small to make properly. I have developed these recipes in larger, easy-to-make quantities. I have suggested the amount you should need for each recipe in the ingredients list for that recipe. However, you can adjust the amounts used to suit your own taste.

green curry paste

kruang gaeng keow-wan

1 teaspoon coriander seeds

1 teaspoon cumin seeds

1 teaspoon white peppercorns

1 tablespoon chopped fresh lemongrass

3 cm fresh galangal or ginger, peeled and chopped

2 long green chillies, chopped

10 small green chillies, chopped

2 tablespoons chopped garlic

3 pink Thai shallots or 2 regular ones, chopped

3 coriander roots, chopped

1 teaspoon chopped kaffir lime skin, or finely chopped lime leaves

2 teaspoons shrimp paste

Using a mortar and pestle, grind all the ingredients to a thick paste.

panaeng curry paste

kruang gaeng panaeng

10 long dried red chillies, deseeded and chopped

5 pink Thai shallots or 3 regular ones, chopped

2 tablespoons chopped garlic

2 stalks of lemongrass, chopped

3 cm fresh galangal or ginger, peeled and chopped

1 teaspoon ground coriander

1 teaspoon ground cumin

3 coriander roots, chopped

1 teaspoon shrimp paste

2 tablespoons roasted peanuts

Using a mortar and pestle, grind all the ingredients into a paste.

Note The recipes make about 6–10 tablespoons paste. If necessary, spoon the remainder into ice cube trays, freeze, then keep in labelled plastic bags for future use. One cube yields about 1 tablespoon paste. In the West, ginger is often substituted for galangal, though it has a different flavour.

red curry paste

kruang gaeng daeng

8 long red dried chillies, deseeded and chopped

1 teaspoon ground coriander seed

½ teaspoon ground cumin seed

1 teaspoon freshly ground white pepper

2 tablespoons chopped garlic

2 stalks of lemongrass, chopped

3 coriander roots, chopped

1 teaspoon chopped kaffir lime skin, or finely chopped lime leaves

3 cm fresh galangal or ginger, peeled and chopped

2 teaspoons shrimp paste

1 teaspoon salt

Using a mortar and pestle, grind all the ingredients into a paste.

massaman curry paste

kruang gaeng massaman

10 long dried red chillies, deseeded and chopped

1 tablespoon ground coriander seeds

1 teaspoon ground cinnamon

1 teaspoon ground cumin seeds

1 teaspoon ground cloves

2 whole star anise

1 teaspoon ground cardamom

1 teaspoon freshly ground white pepper

6 pink Thai shallots or 3 regular, chopped

7 garlic cloves, chopped

5 cm fresh lemongrass, chopped

1 cm fresh galangal or ginger, peeled and chopped

1 tablespoon chopped kaffir lime skin or finely chopped lime leaves

1 tablespoon shrimp paste

1 tablespoon salt

Using a mortar and pestle, grind the dried spices. Add the remaining ingredients, blending after each addition, to form a paste.

websites, oriental markets and mail order

Amaranth Thai Market
346 Garratt Lane, London SW18 4ES
Tel: 020 8871 3466
www.amaranthcuisine.com

Chuanglee Thai Provision
Unit 1/271 Merton Road,
London SW18 5JS
Tel: 020 8870 5292

**Cheung's Oriental
Supermarket**
270 Wandsworth Road,
London SW8 2JR
Tel: 020 7622 9880

Filipino Supermarket
1 Kenway Road, London SW5 0RP
Tel: 020 7244 1111

Golden Gate Supermarket
16 Newport Place, London WC2H 7PR
Tel: 020 7437 0014

**Good Harvest Fish and
Meat Market**
14 Newport Place, London WC2H 7PR
Tel: 020 7437 0712

HOO HING STORES
www.hoohing.com/stores
*Oriental supermarkets carrying
many Thai brands. Shop in person
or on-line. Stores listed below:*

• Hoo Hing North London
Lockfield Avenue, Off Mollison
Avenue, Brimsdown, Enfield,
Middlesex EN3 7Q
Tel: 020 8344 9888

• Hoo Hing South London
Bond Road, Off Western Road,
Mitcham, Surrey CR4 3EB
Tel: 020 8687 2633

• Hoo Hing East London
Unit A, Eastway Commercial Centre,
Eastway, London E9 5NR
Tel: 020 8533 2811

• Hoo Hing West London
A406 North Circular Road, Near
Hangar Lane Park Royal,
London NW10 7TN
Tel: 020 8838 3388

• Hoo Hing Essex
Hoo Hing Commercial Centre,
Freshwater Road, Chadwell Heath,
Romford, Essex RM8 1RX
Tel: 020 8548 3677

Lai Loi Oriental
180 Deptford High Street,
London, SE8 3PR
Tel: 020 8691 1883

Loon Fung Supermarket
42 Gerrard Street, London W1D 5QJ
Tel: 020 7437 7332
*One of the best-known Oriental
supermarkets in London.*

Manila Supermarket
11 Hogarth Place, London SW5 0QT
Tel: 020 7373 8305
Filipino and Thai food.

New Loon Moon Supermarket
9 Gerrard Street, London W1D 5PP
Tel: 020 7734 3887
*Authentic food from China, Korea,
Malaysia, Thailand and the
Philippines. Excellent range of Thai
spice pastes and other ingredients,
fresh, packaged, canned or frozen.
Also Asian cooking utensils.*

Newport Supermarket
32 Newport Court,
London WC2H 7PQ
Tel: 020 7437 2536
*Chinese, Indonesian, Japanese,
Korean, Thai.*

Oriental City
(formerly Yaohan Plaza)
399 Edgware Road, Colindale,
London NW9 0JJ
Tel: 020 8200 0009
*London's largest Oriental shopping
mall. The supermarket sells a wide
selection of foods from Japan, Korea,
Thailand, Hong Kong, Malaysia,
Singapore and India. Also in the mall
is an Oriental Cook Shop, bookstore
and other stores selling tableware.*

Rumwong Thai Market
20 London Road, Guildford, Surrey
GU1 2AF
Tel: 01483 599499
*Fresh Thai ingredients, curry pastes,
sauces, canned foods and porcelain.*

See Woo Hong Supermarket
20 Lisle Street,
London WC2H 7BA
Tel: 020 7439 8325
*Excellent source of utensils,
tableware and ingredients.*

See Woo Cash and Carry
108 Horn Lane, Greenwich,
London SE10 0RT
Tel: 020 8293 9393
*A wide range of live seafood kept in
tanks.*

Sri Thai Supermarket
56 Shepherd's Bush Road,
London W6 7PH
Tel: 020 7602 0621

Talad Thai
320 Upper Richmond Road,
London SW15 6TL
Tel: 020 8789 8084

Tawana (Thai)
16–18 Chepstow Road,
London W2 5BD
Tel: 020 7221 6316

Thai4uk
www.thai4uk.com
*Web-based shop selling Thai
ingredients direct.*

Wang Thai Supermarket
101 Kew Road, Surrey TW9 2PN
Tel: 020 8332 2959

WING TAI SUPERMARKETS
*A large range of foodstuffs from
China, Japan, Korea, Thailand and
Vietnam.*

• Wing Tai Supermarket
Unit 11a, Aylesham Centre,
London, SE15 5EW
Tel: 020 7635 0714
Fax: 020 7635 6920

• Wing Tai Supermarket II
13 Electric Avenue, Brixton,
London SW9 8JY
Tel: 020 7738 5898

WING YIP SUPERSTORES
*Four Chinese superstores with a
vast selection of Chinese, Japanese,
Thai, Malaysian and Indonesian
foods and cooking utensils.*

• Wing Yip Centre
375 Nechells Park Road, Nechells,
Birmingham B7 5NT
Tel: 0121 327 6618
Fax: 0121 327 6612

• Wing Yip Cricklewood
395 Edgware Road, Cricklewood
NW2 6LN
Tel: 020 8450 0422
Fax: 020 8452 1478

• Wing Yip Croydon
544 Purley Way, Croydon CR0 4RF
Tel: 020 8688 4880
Fax: 020 8688 8786

• Wing Yip Manchester
Oldham Road, Ancoats,
Manchester M4 5HU
Tel: 0161 832 3215
Fax: 0161 832 2794

COCKTAIL CRAB CLAWS
AND OTHER SEAFOOD

The Fish Society
www.thefishsociety.co.uk
*High-quality mail order fish and
other seafood, on an amusing
website.*

Island Seafare Limited
Alfred Pier, Port St Mary,
Isle of Man IM9 5EF
Tel: 01624 834494
Fax: 01624 835550
www.islandseafare.co.uk
*Sells shucked frozen cocktail crab
claws mail order.*

Shetland Norse
Mid Yell, Shetland ZE2 9BN
Tel: 01957 702112
Fax: 01957 702088
www.shetlandnorse.co.uk
Sells cocktail crab claws mail order.

index